APPLICATIONS WORKBOOK

Fourth Edition

Procedures for the Office Professional

Patsy Fulton-Calkins, Ph.D., CPS
Adjunct Professor
Educational Consultant

Joanna D. Hanks
Dean of Instructional Services
J. Sargeant Reynolds Community College
Richmond, Virginia

Contributing Author

Karin M. Stultz
Northern Michigan University
Marquette, Michigan

VISIT US ON THE INTERNET
www.swep.com
www.thomsonlearning.com

South-Western
EDUCATIONAL PUBLISHING
Thomson Learning™

Australia • Canada • Denmark • Japan • Mexico • New Zealand • Phillipines
Puerto Rico • Singapore • South Africa • Spain • United Kingdom • United States

PREFACE

To the Student

This workbook provides additional materials that you will need in completing assignments in your text, plus the following items.

- Supplemental exercises for each chapter
- Six vocabulary reviews (one relating to each section of the text)
- A language skills practice in which you will have an opportunity to practice using the language usage rules presented in the Reference Section of your text
- A simulated office activity that includes several tasks, presented over a period of five days

Your Company

You work for People First International. The company is a full-service agency that places people in positions in the United States, France, and Germany. Its offices are located in cities listed below in the United States and Europe.

- Detroit, Michigan (home office)
- New York City, New York
- Atlanta, Georgia
- Paris, France
- Frankfurt, Germany

People First International is a relatively young company; its first office was opened in 1988 in Detroit, Michigan (the home office). In 1990, the New York City office was opened, followed by the Atlanta office in 1992, the Paris office in 1995, and the Frankfurt office in 1997. The company places people in full-time, part-time, or contracted positions.

Vision/Value Statement for People First International

People First International is a service organization. Our major responsibility is to provide quality services to our worldwide clients. We constantly strive to provide these services in a timely manner and at a reasonable price. We are responsible to our employees and to the worldwide communities where we live and work. We value:

- Continual learning
- Integrity
- Diversity
- Creativity

Your Position

You are an administrative assistant to Juan Menendez, Vice President of International Operations. Your office is in Detroit. Your office hours are from 8:30 a.m. to 5:00 p.m; however, you are expected to work overtime when your workload demands it. Your job responsibilities are diverse, including preparing correspondence, making travel arrangements, conference arrangements, and communicating with the offices in Paris and Frankfurt. You also travel occasionally to the offices in Paris and Frankfurt to help in the orientation and training of new employees. You speak both French and German.

You supervise one office professional, Roger VanDorn, who has been with the company for six months.

You recently were elected to the vice presidency of IAAP. Before you accepted the position, you discussed the possibility with Mr. Menendez. He was extremely supportive of your accepting the role; he believes strongly in continued professional growth and employees of People First contributing to the community in which they live. He made it clear that he would support your performing some of your duties for IAAP while you are at work; he does want to know approximately how many hours per week you are giving to IAAP. Your agreement was that the two of you will review the hours spent on IAAP work each month. He will let you know if he believes the hours have become excessive. You are not to use any company stationery or supplies; however, you may use the company copier for limited copies and the company fax and email for limited correspondence.

CONTENTS

To complete certain Office Applications given in your text, *Procedures for the Office Professional,* you must use information and forms that are provided in this workbook. The Office Applications and Supplemental Exercises that require the use of this workbook are identified below. Each individual office application or supplemental exercise is identified by the appropriate number at the top and bottom of each sheet.

CONTENTS

DIRECTIONS: Using the information given here, prepare a chart showing graphically the percent of the labor force by race for 1996 and projected for 2006. Provide an appropriate title for the chart and hand in one copy to your instructor.

Labor Force	1996	2006
White	77 percent	74 percent
Hispanic	9 percent	11 percent
Black	10 percent	10 percent
Asian	4 percent	5 percent

OA 1-4 (GOAL 3)

DIRECTIONS: To help you understand what your strengths and weaknesses are, rate yourself using the self-evaluation chart below. Discuss your evaluation with a trusted friend, coworker, or family member to see if the person agrees with your ratings. Keep your self-evaluation; you will rate yourself again at the end of the course to determine if you have improved.

SELF-EVALUATION CHART

These questions are intended to help you examine personality and character traits. In Column 1 answer each question with "yes," "no," or "sometimes." You will complete Column 2 when you refer back to this chart in a later chapter. Notice the questions where you answered "yes." These are probably areas of strength. The questions where you answered "sometimes" or "no" may be areas needing improvement. Write two paragraphs describing your strengths and two paragraphs on traits you would like to improve. In a final paragraph, include the steps you intend to take to make improvement in these areas. When you refer back to this chart in several months, you will assess your progress.

	Column 1	Column 2
CONFIDENCE AND COURAGE		
• Do you have confidence in your skills and abilities?		
• Do you stand up for what you think is right?		
• Do you continue to try in spite of failures?		
POISE		
• Are you patient with others?		
• Do you value high moral and ethical standards?		
INITIATIVE AND AMBITION		
• Do you make decisions instead of relying on others?		
• Do you do more than is expected of you?		
• Do you make good use of your spare time?		
• Do you take pride in doing good work?		
KNOWLEDGE AND JUDGMENT		
• Do you like to learn new things?		
• Do you ask questions about things you do not understand?		
• Do you think before you act?		
DEPENDABILITY		
• Are you punctual?		
• Can you be counted on to get a job done?		
• Do you follow through on promises you make?		
INTEGRITY		
• Are you trustworthy?		
• Do you respect the opinion of others?		
• Are you faithful in performing what is expected of you?		
GETTING ALONG WITH OTHERS		
• Do you listen attentively when someone is talking?		
• Do you try to find something good in everyone?		
• Are you cheerful?		
• Do you avoid criticizing others?		
DETERMINATION AND PERSEVERANCE		
• Do you stay with a job until it is finished?		
• Are you the type of person who isn't discouraged easily?		
• Do you willingly accept difficult assignments?		

Chapter 1 Supplemental Exercise

DIRECTIONS: The following paragraphs provide information on the training and qualifications needed for clerical supervisors and managers, court reporters and medical transcriptionists, record clerks, and secretaries. Prepare the information in columnar form, showing the training and qualifications needed for each occupational area. Provide an appropriate title for your summary; submit the information to your instructor.

Clerical Supervisors and Managers

Training and Qualifications

To be eligible for promotion to a supervisory position, clerical or administrative support workers must prove they are capable of handling additional responsibilities. When evaluating candidates, superiors look for strong teamwork skills, determination, loyalty, poise, and confidence. They also look for more specific supervisory attributes, such as the ability to organize and coordinate work efficiently, set priorities, and motivate others. Increasingly, supervisors need a broad base of office skills coupled with personal flexibility to adapt to changes in organizational structure and move among departments when necessary. In addition, supervisors must pay close attention to detail in order to identify and correct errors made by subordinates. Good working knowledge of the organization's computer system is also an advantage. Many employers require postsecondary training—in some cases, an associate's or a bachelor's degree.

Court Reporters and Medical Transcriptionists

Training and Qualifications

Court reporters generally complete a two- or four-year training program, offered by about 300 postsecondary vocational and technical schools and colleges. About 110 programs have been approved by the National Court Reporters Association, all of which teach computer-aided transcription and real-time reporting. NCRA-approved programs require students to capture 225 words per minute. Court reporters in the Federal Government generally must capture at least 205 words a minute.

Some states require court reporters to be notary publics or to be a Certified Court Reporter. Reporters must pass a state certification test administered by a board of examiners to earn this designation. The National Court Reporters Association confers the designation Registered Professional Reporter (RPR) on those who pass a two-part examination and participate in continuing education programs. Although voluntary, the RPR designation is recognized as a mark of distinction in this field.

For medical transcriptionist jobs, understanding medical terminology is essential. Good English grammar and punctuation skills are required, as well as familiarity with personal computers and word processing software. Good listening skills are also necessary, because some doctors and health-care professionals speak English as a second language.

Employers prefer to hire transcriptionists who have completed postsecondary training in medical transcription, offered by many vocational schools and community colleges. Completion of a two-year associate's degree program—including coursework in anatomy, medical terminology, medical/legal issues, and English grammar and punctuation—is highly recommended. The American Association for Medical Transcriptionists awards the voluntary designation Certified Medical Transcriptionist (CMT) to those who earn passing scores on written and practical examinations. As in many other fields, certification is recognized as a sign of competence in medical transcription. To retain this credential, CMT's must obtain at least 30 continuing education credits every three years.

Record Clerks
Training and Qualifications

Most record clerk jobs are entry-level, with most employers requiring applicants to have at least a high school diploma or its equivalent. A higher level of education is usually favored over a high school diploma. Brokerage firms increasingly seek college graduates, and order clerks in high-technology firms often need to understand scientific and mechanical processes, which may require some college education. Regardless of the type of work, most employers prefer workers who are computer literate. Knowledge of word processing and spreadsheet software is especially valuable, as are experience working in an office and good interpersonal skills.

Business education programs in business schools and community colleges typically include courses in keyboarding, word processing, shorthand, business communications, records management, and office systems and procedures. Technical training needed for some specialized order clerk positions can be obtained in technical institutes and in two- and four-year colleges.

Some entrants into the record clerk field are college graduates with degrees in business, finance, or liberal arts. Although a degree is rarely required, many graduates accept entry-level clerical positions to get into a particular company or to enter the finance or accounting field, with the hope of being promoted to professional or managerial jobs.

Records clerks must be careful, orderly, and detail oriented in order to avoid making errors and to be able to recognize errors made by others. These workers also must be honest, discreet, and trustworthy because they frequently come in contact with confidential material. Additionally, payroll clerks; billing clerks; and bookkeeping, accounting, and auditing clerks should have a strong aptitude for numbers. Because statement clerks have access to individuals' financial information, these workers must be bonded.

Secretaries

Training and Qualifications

High school graduates may qualify for secretarial positions provided they have basic office skills. Secretaries should be proficient in keyboarding and good at spelling, punctuation, grammar, and oral communication. Knowledge of word processing, spreadsheet and database management programs is becoming increasingly important to most employers. Because secretaries must be tactful in their dealings with many different people, employers also look for good interpersonal skills. Discretion, judgment, organizational ability, and initiative are especially important for higher level secretarial positions.

As office automation continues to evolve, retraining and continuing education will remain an integral part of many jobs. Continuing changes in the office environment have increased the demand for secretaries who are adaptable and versatile. Secretaries may have to attend classes to learn to operate new office equipment such as word processing equipment, information storage systems, personal computers, or new updated software programs.

Secretarial training ranges from high school vocational education programs that teach office practices and other skills to business schools, vocational-technical institutes, and community colleges.

Advancement for secretaries generally comes about by promotion to a secretarial position with more responsibilities. Qualified secretaries who broaden their knowledge of the company's operations and enhance their skills may be promoted to other positions such as senior or executive secretary, clerical supervisor, or office manager.

Source: U.S. Department of Labor, *Occupational Outlook Handbook* (Washington, D.C.: Bureau of Labor Statistics, 1998–99), 278, 288, 296.

OA2-4 (GOAL 3)

DIRECTIONS: Here is the draft of an article for People First International's newsletter. Cecilia Ivon, the company's president, coauthored the article with Hugh Minor, vice president of communications. Key the article in an appropriate format. There is a rough draft of an organization chart. Notice that it is not a traditional organization chart—customers are listed at the top of the chart, with the president at the bottom. Using graphics, present this chart in an attractive and creative format. Submit the article, along with the organization chart to your instructor.

All caps [**On Better Communications. . .** *Double space*
Cecelia Ivon and Hugh Minor

Put this in italics{ The effectiveness of your life is determined by the effectiveness of your communication skills.

This adage sounds simple, but it is so true. Companies fail, relationships end, and sales are lost because people do not—or cannot—communicate effectively. We must routinely and consistently share ~~out~~ our thoughts with each other so that we eliminate any confusion or misunderstanding.

Put in a box if possible

Question: Are The best communicators ~~are~~ the best talkers?

italics The answer is No! The best communicators are those who (listen) attentively. Too often hearing is ~~listening~~ confused with ~~hearing.~~ hearing involves detecting sound vibrations; listening means making sense from what we hear.

Listening requires paying attention, interperting what we hear, and remember ^ing important facts.

Let's *reword this* -

Externally we communicate with our customers, vendors, and the general public.

We need to consider effective communication skills both internally and externally. We communicate internally with our fellow team members. External communication is involves talking with our customers, vendors, and the general public. Our goal is to improve communication in both areas.

In communicating there are words that negatively impact our message. Some of these words and phrases are listed below.

1. That's not my job (or department)
2. Can't
3. But
4. It's policy
5. Problem

People like to be around people who openly communicate and who are sincerely interested in what they are saying. Good communicators are people-oriented. It takes hard work and practice to be a good communicator-but we owe it to ourselves and our customers.

Likewise, there are words that have a positive effect on a message. Some of these words are listed here.

1. I appreciate
2. Please
3. Opportunity
4. Thank you
5. How can I help

(figure 1)

By using the inverted pyramid philosophy and placing the customer at the top of the organization, employees become empowered and supported by their managers to do their absolute best in communicating internally and externally.

ORGANIZATIONAL STRUCTURE

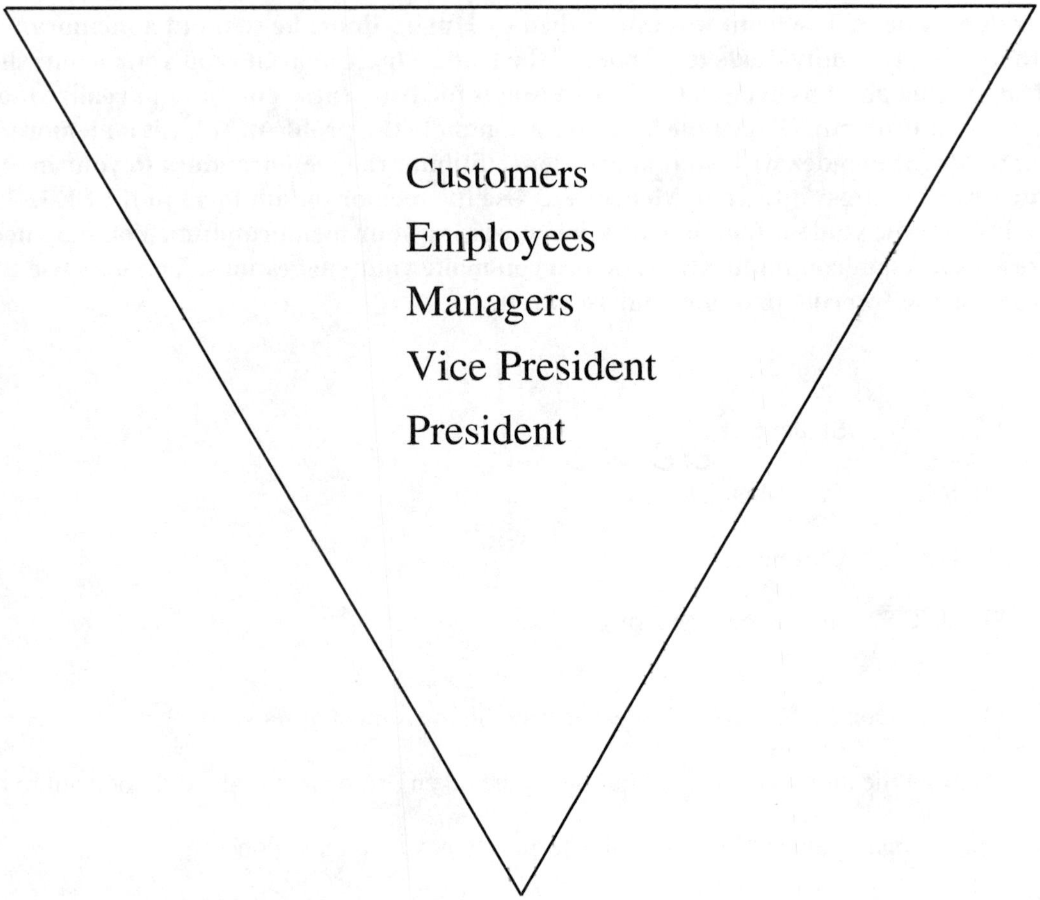

Customers
Employees
Managers
Vice President
President

Figure 1

Chapter 2 Supplemental Exercise

DIRECTIONS: You find the following note from Juan Menendez on your desk. You have been chairing a communications team designed to improve communications in your department. The team was established by Hugh Minor; he sent out a memorandum inviting the individuals to be part of the team. Mao Chanren is on your team; she is from China and has been in the United States for two years. You did not realize that there was a problem. Determine how you will handle the problem; submit a memorandum to Mr. Menendez with your suggestions. (Submit the memorandum to your instructor but address it to Juan Menendez.) Use the memorandum form in file SE02-1 provided on the student template disk when writing your memorandum. You may need to research Asian communications before you make your suggestions. You may use the library or the Internet in doing your research.

TO: Student

FROM: Juan Menendez

DATE: Current

SUBJECT: Employee Concern

Mao Chanren came in to see me yesterday. She was most upset with what is happening on the Communications Team and requested to be taken off the team. She did not want to tell me the problems; but when I insisted, she hesitantly gave me these concerns.

- She was criticized by one of the team members during a meeting.

- A team member asked her to voice an opinion on a situation that she felt uncomfortable talking about before the entire team.

- She was asked by a team member to talk with another person outside the team about an issue. She said that she would do so; however, she did not because she did not feel comfortable talking with the person. You asked her for a report of her findings at the next meeting. She did not have a report.

I want to keep her on the team. She is a very good worker and extremely intelligent. We need to help her feel a part of People First. What suggestions do you have for dealing with these issues and making her feel a part of the team? Please let me know within the next week.

OA3-2 (GOALS 2 AND 3)

STRESS AUDIT

DIRECTIONS: Respond to the items given here. Score your Stress Audit by using the points given at the end of the Stress Audit. Then, prepare an action plan, using the form given on the student template disk in file OA03-2. List the steps you will take in an attempt to reduce your stress level. Do not turn in these items to your instructor. Make a commitment to reducing your stress while in this course. Keep your Stress Audit. At the end of the course, you will retake the Stress Audit to determine if you have been able to reduce your stress.

1. You are upset by your partner's or colleague's behavior. Do you

   a. Blow up.
   b. Feel angry but suppress it.
   c. Feel upset but do not get angry.
   d. Cry.
   e. None of the above.

2. You must get through a mountain of work in one morning. Do you

   a. Work extra hard and complete the lot.
   b. Forget the work and make yourself a drink.
   c. Do as much as you can.
   d. Prioritize the load and complete only the most important tasks.
   e. Ask someone to help you.

3. You overhear a conversation in which a friend or colleague makes some unkind remarks about you. Do you

   a. Interrupt the conversation and give him or her a piece of your mind.
   b. Walk straight by without giving it much thought.
   c. Walk straight by and think about getting even.
   d. Walk straight by but sulk about it.

4. You are stuck in heavy traffic. Do you

   a. Sound your horn.
   b. Try to drive down a side road to avoid the jam.
   c. Switch on the radio, cassette, or CD.
   d. Sit back and try to relax.
   e. Sit back and feel angry.
   f. Get on with some work.
   g. The question does not apply because you do not have a car.

5. When you play a sport, do you play to win

   a. Always.
   b. Most of the time.
   c. Sometimes.
   d. Never. I just play for the game.

6. When you play a game with children do you deliberately let them win

   a. Never. They've got to learn.
   b. Sometimes.
   c. Most of the time.
   d. Always. It is only a game.

7. You are working on a project. The deadline is approaching fast but the work is not quite right. Do you

    a. Work on it all night and day to make sure it's perfect.
    b. Start to panic because you think you will not complete it in time.
    c. Present your best in the time available without losing sleep over it.

8. Someone else tidies up your room/office/garage/workshop and never places the items/furniture back in the original place. Do you

    a. Mark the position of each item and ask the person to put it back exactly where it should be.
    b. Move everything back to its original position after the person has gone.
    c. Leave most things as they are—you do not mind the occasional shift around.

9. A close friend asks for your opinion about a newly decorated room. Do you

    a. Think it's awful and say so.
    b. Think it's awful but say it looks wonderful.
    c. Think it's awful but comment about the good aspects.
    d. Think it's awful and suggest improvements.

10. When you do something do you

    a. Always work to produce a perfect result.
    b. Do your best and do not worry if it is not perfect.
    c. Think that everything you do is perfect.

11. Your family complains that you spend too little time with them because of your work. Do you

    a. Worry but feel that you cannot do anything about it.
    b. Work in the family room so that you can be with them.
    c. Take on more work.
    d. Find that your family has never complained.
    e. Reorganize your work so that you can be with them more.

12. What is your idea of an ideal evening?

    a. A large party with lots to drink and eat.
    b. An evening with your partner doing something you both enjoy.
    c. Getting away from it all by yourself.
    d. A small group of friends at dinner.
    e. An evening with the family doing something you all enjoy.
    f. Working.

13. Which one or more of the following do you do?

    a. Bite your nails.
    b. Feel constantly tired.
    c. Feel breathless without exertion.
    d. Drum with your fingers.
    e. Sweat for no apparent reason.
    f. Fidget.
    g. Gesticulate
    h. None of the above.

14. Which one or more of the following do you suffer from?

    a. Headaches.
    b. Muscle tenseness.
    c. Constipation.
    d. Diarrhea.
    e. Loss of appetite.
    f. Increase in appetite.
    g. None of the above.

15. Has one or more of the following happened to you during the last month?

    a. Crying or the desire to cry.
    b. Difficulty in concentrating.
    c. Forgetting what you were going to say next.
    d. Little things irritating you.
    e. Difficulty in making decisions.
    f. Wanting to scream.
    g. Feeling that there is no one with whom you can really talk.
    h. Finding that you are rushing on to another task before you have finished the first one.
    i. I have not experienced any of the above.

16. Have you experienced any of the following during the last year?

    a. A serious illness to yourself or someone close to you.
    b. Problems with your family.
    c. Financial problems.
    d. None of the above.

17. How many cigarettes do you smoke each day?

    a. None.
    b. One to ten.
    c. Eleven to twenty.
    d. Twenty-one or more.

18. How much alcohol do you drink a day?

    a. None.
    b. One or two drinks.
    c. Three to five drinks.
    d. Six or more drinks.

19. How many cups of freshly brewed (not decaffeinated) coffee do you drink a day?

    a. None.
    b. One or two cups.
    c. Three to five cups.
    d. Six or more cups.

20. How old are you?

    a. 18 or below.
    b. 19–25.
    c. 26–39.
    d. 40–65.
    e. 66 or over.

21. You have a very important appointment at 9:30 a.m. Do you

    a. Have a sleepless night worrying about it.
    b. Sleep well and wake up fairly relaxed but thinking about the appointment.
    c. Sleep well and wake up looking forward to the appointment.

22. Someone close to you has died. Of course you are very upset. Do you

    a. Grieve because no one can ever fill that awful gap.
    b. Grieve because life is so unfair.
    c. Accept what has happened and try to get on with your life.

23. You are in deep water over a problem. Do you

    a. Reassess the situation by yourself and try to work something else out.
    b. Talk over the problem with your partner or close friend and work something out.
    c. Deny that there is a problem in the hope that the worst may never happen.
    d. Worry about it and do nothing to try to solve it.

24. When did you last smile?

    a. Today.
    b. Yesterday.
    c. Last week.
    d. Cannot remember.

25. When did you last compliment or praise someone—your children, your partner, colleagues, friends?

    a. Today.
    b. Yesterday.
    c. Last week.
    d. Cannot remember.

Source: Looker, Terry and Olga Gregson, *Managing Stress* (Chicago: NTC Publishing Group, 1997), 11–15. Reprinted with permission from Hodder and Stoughton, London, England.

SCORE YOUR STRESS AUDIT

Now note down your score for each question and add them up.

 1. a = 0 b = 0 c = 3 d = 0 e = 1
 2. a = 1 b = 0 c = 1 d = 3 e = 2
 3. a = 0 b = 3 c = 0 d = 1
 4. a = 0 b = 0 c = 2 d = 3 e = 0 f = 2 g = 1
 5. a = 0 b = 1 c = 2 d = 3
 6. a = 0 b = 1 c = 2 d = 3
 7. a = 0 b = 0 c = 3
 8. a = 0 b = 0 c = 3
 9. a = 0 b = 0 c = 3 d = 1
10. a = 0 b = 3 c = 0
11. a = 0 b = 0 c = 0 d = 0 e = 3
12. a = 1 b = 3 c = 0 d = 1 e = 2 f = 0
13. a = 0 b = 0 c = 0 d = 0 e = 0 f = 0 g = 0 h = 1
14. a = 0 b = 0 c = 0 d = 0 e = 0 f = 0 g = 1
15. a = 0 b = 0 c = 0 d = 0 e = 0 f = 0 g = 0 h = 0 I = 1
16. a = 0 b = 0 c = 0 d = 2
17. a = 3 b = 1 c = 0 d = 0
18. a = 3 b = 2 c = 1 d = 0
19. a = 3 b = 2 c = 1 d = 0
20. a = 0 b = 0 c = 1 d = 2 e = 3
21. a = 0 b = 1 c = 3
22. a = 0 b = 0 c = 3
23. a = 2 b = 3 c = 0 d = 0
24. a = 3 b = 2 c = 1 d = 0
25. a = 3 b = 2 c = 1 d = 0

EVALUATION

51–68: Your stress level is low. You show very few signs of stress.
33–50: Your stress level is moderate. You show some stress.
16–32: Your stress level is high. You may show many signs of stress.
0–15: Your stress level is very high. You show a great deal of stress.

OA3-4 (GOAL 3)

DIRECTIONS: Using the forms provided here, log the time you spend in various activities on the forms. Record each day's activities on a different form. If you are employed, log the time you spend in activities at work. If you are not employed, log the way you use your personal time.

Analyze the way you spent your time during the five days by answering the questions on the Time Management Analysis on page 23. Using the Action Plan form on the student template disk in file OA03-4, prepare an action plan listing techniques you will use to better manage your time. Submit your action plan to your instructor.

DAILY TIME LOG

Name _____ Day _____ Date _____

Time	Activity	Priority*	Interruptions (nature of)
		1 2 3	
		1 2 3	
		1 2 3	
		1 2 3	
		1 2 3	
		1 2 3	
		1 2 3	
		1 2 3	
		1 2 3	
		1 2 3	
		1 2 3	
		1 2 3	

*Circle the number which indicates the importance of the activity. Priority code:

1 – Urgent, 2 – Do today, and 3 – Do when convenient

DAILY TIME LOG

Name _____ Day _____ Date _____

Time	Activity	Priority*	Interruptions (nature of)
		1 2 3	
		1 2 3	
		1 2 3	
		1 2 3	
		1 2 3	
		1 2 3	
		1 2 3	
		1 2 3	
		1 2 3	
		1 2 3	
		1 2 3	
		1 2 3	

*Circle the number which indicates the importance of the activity. Priority code:

1 – Urgent, 2 – Do today, and 3 – Do when convenient

DAILY TIME LOG

Name _____ Day _____ Date _____

Time	Activity	Priority*	Interruptions (nature of)
		1 2 3	
		1 2 3	
		1 2 3	
		1 2 3	
		1 2 3	
		1 2 3	
		1 2 3	
		1 2 3	
		1 2 3	
		1 2 3	
		1 2 3	
		1 2 3	

*Circle the number which indicates the importance of the activity. Priority code:

1 – Urgent, 2 – Do today, and 3 – Do when convenient

OA 3-4

DAILY TIME LOG

Name _____ Day _____ Date _____

Time	Activity	Priority*	Interruptions (nature of)
		1 2 3	
		1 2 3	
		1 2 3	
		1 2 3	
		1 2 3	
		1 2 3	
		1 2 3	
		1 2 3	
		1 2 3	
		1 2 3	
		1 2 3	
		1 2 3	

*Circle the number which indicates the importance of the activity. Priority code:

1 – Urgent, 2 – Do today, and 3 – Do when convenient

DAILY TIME LOG

Name _____ Day _____ Date _____

Time	Activity	Priority*	Interruptions (nature of)
		1 2 3	
		1 2 3	
		1 2 3	
		1 2 3	
		1 2 3	
		1 2 3	
		1 2 3	
		1 2 3	
		1 2 3	
		1 2 3	
		1 2 3	
		1 2 3	

*Circle the number which indicates the importance of the activity. Priority code:

1 – Urgent, 2 – Do today, and 3 – Do when convenient

TIME MANAGEMENT ANALYSIS

DIRECTIONS: Analyze the way you spent your time during the three days you made recordings in the time logs. Answer these questions:

1. What patterns and habits are apparent from the time log?

    _____

    _____

2. What was the most productive period of the day?

    _____

3. What was the least productive period of the day?

    _____

4. Who or what accounted for the interruptions?

    _____

5. Can the interruptions be controlled or minimized?

    _____

    _____

6. What were the biggest time wasters?

    _____

    _____

7. How can the time wasters be eliminated or minimized?

    _____

    _____

8. On what activities can less time be spent?

    _____

    _____

9. What activities need more time?

    _____

    _____

Chapter 3 Supplemental Exercise

DIRECTIONS: Read the case given here. Respond in the space provided to the three items at the end of the case. Share your responses in a small group discussion with your class members.

Chang Timms works as a systems analyst for People First International. He reports to Dianne Bradwell. Chang was assigned a major project two months ago; it is due next month.

Recently Dianne's workload has increased dramatically since a new computer system was installed throughout the agency. Dianne has been calling Chang to "troubleshoot" problems with the computer system as they are reported to her office. Of course, these problems must be dealt with immediately, since employees may be unable to continue their work if the system is down.

Chang had been planning to take two weeks' vacation soon, but he has gotten behind on the project that is due next month. In fact, he has at least six weeks of work left on the project, and he has only four weeks to finish. He feels "burned out" due to his heavy workload. He tries to work on the project every day, but Dianne's calls have kept him busy. He has not mentioned to Dianne that he is behind on the project. Recently he has even given up taking lunch hours. He brings a sandwich from home and works through lunch.

Analyze Chang's work habits and their effect on his productivity. Prepare written responses to the following questions, and then share your thoughts in small group discussions.

1. Describe what may result if Chang continues to handle his situation as he currently is.

_____

_____

_____

_____

_____

_____

2. How can Chang manage his time more efficiently?

_____

_____

_____

_____

_____

3. Does he need to talk to his supervisor about the situation? If so, what does he say to her?

_____

_____

_____

_____

_____

Chapter 4 Supplemental Exercise 1

DIRECTIONS: Ethical behavior is defined as doing what is right regardless of expected profit. Ethical organizations treat people fairly and respect cultural differences. Office professionals, as well as all employees, regularly face situations that call for ethical decisions. Read each of the following statements. Place a check mark under "agree" or "disagree" to represent your honest opinion of what you believe is ethically right in each situation. After you complete the form, discuss your answers with your classmates in groups of three or four.

	Agree	*Disagree*
1. You must follow your supervisor's instruction to "lose" a file that the federal auditors ask to see.	_____	_____
2. Making a personal long-distance telephone call on your office's bill is acceptable if others in the company follow this practice.	_____	_____
3. You should say that a culturally biased joke is offensive and walk away if someone persists in this practice.	_____	_____
4. Telling your best friend (who is not employed by your firm) about the personal relationships of your coworkers has no impact on the company's business.	_____	_____
5. You should report a coworker who takes office supplies home for her personal business.	_____	_____
6. It is permissible to use a day of sick leave (especially because you have earned it) for going on a beach trip with your friends.	_____	_____
7. The representative of a firm (that has a major contract with your company) should be reported for making sexually suggestive comments to you.	_____	_____

Chapter 4 Supplemental Exercise 2

DIRECTIONS: You are to work in teams of three or four on this assignment. Develop a Credo for a company where you would like to work. You may use the Johnson & Johnson Credo, given below, as a resource. Once the Credo has been developed, key it in an attractive format, using graphics. Submit your Credo to your instructor.

JOHNSON & JOHNSON CREDO

We believe our first responsibility is to the doctors, nurses and patients,
to mothers and fathers and all others who use our products and services.
In meeting their needs everything we do must be of high quality.
We must constantly strive to reduce our costs
in order to maintain reasonable prices.
Customers' orders must be serviced promptly and accurately.
Our suppliers and distributors must have an opportunity
to make a fair profit.

We are responsible to our employees,
the men and women who work with us throughout the world.
Everyone must be considered as an individual.
We must respect their dignity and recognize their merit.
They must have a sense of security in their jobs.
Compensation must be fair and adequate,
and working conditions clean, orderly and safe.
We must be mindful of ways to help our employees fulfill
their family responsibilities.
Employees must feel free to make suggestions and complaints.
There must be equal opportunity for employment, development and advancement for those qualified.
We must provide competent management,
and their actions must be just and ethical.

We are responsible to the communities in which we live and work
and to the world community as well.
We must be good citizens—support good works and charities
and bear our fair share of taxes.
We must encourage civic improvements and better health and education.
We must maintain in good order
the property we are privileged to use,
protecting the environment and natural resources.

Our final responsibility is to our stockholders.
Business must make a sound profit.
We must experiment with new ideas.
Research must be carried on, innovative programs provided
and mistakes paid for.
New equipment must be purchased, new facilities provided
and new products launched.
Reserves must be created to provide for adverse times.
When we operate according to these principles,
the stockholders should realize a fair return.

Source: www@http://www.jnj.com.

VOCABULARY REVIEW: PART 1 (CHAPTERS 1–4)

DIRECTIONS: Complete the sentences below by supplying the correct word(s). Submit a copy to your instructor.

1. When work can be performed anywhere and at any time using technology, it is called _____.

2. An organization that implements continuous improvement in the quality of its products and services is said to be practicing _____.

3. When two or more part-time employees perform a job that otherwise one full-time employee would hold, it is referred to as _____.

4. The type of purposeful thinking in which the thinker systematically chooses conscious and deliberate inquiry is referred to as _____.

5. The ability or the power to cause to exist is referred to as _____.

6. Principles and qualities that you consider important are referred to as _____.

7. Skill and grace in dealing with others is referred to as _____.

8. Utilizing an outside company to complete a portion or all of a project is called _____ _____.

9. When communication within a company flows from coworker to coworker and from manager to manager, it is called _____.

10. The bringing together of the physiological factors that make an effective work environment and the psychological factors that explain how workers react to their environment is called _____.

11. The response of the body to a demand made upon it is referred to as _____.

12. When a distressful situation is prolonged with no rest or recuperation for the body, an individual experiences _____.

13. When an individual has inadequate information about his or her work role, there is _____.

14. Reducing the number of employees within an organization is referred to as _____ _____.

15. A resource that cannot be bought, sold, rented, borrowed, saved, or manufactured is referred to as _____.

16. A chronological record of items to be completed is called a _____.

17. The systematic study of moral conduct, duty, and judgment is referred to as _____ _____.

18. Consistently adhering to a set of ideas of right and wrong is called _____.

19. The ideas, customs, values, and skills of a particular organization are defined as
_____.

20. Perceptions or images held of people or things that are derived from selective perception
is defined as _____.

21. A system of negative beliefs and feelings is defined as _____.

22. When a person lacks moral judgment or sensibility, he or she is referred to as _____
_____.

23. The Latin phrase that means "this for that" is _____.

24. A prejudiced view based on background or experiences is defined as _____
_____.

25. The trustworthiness of business to assume accountability for the impact it has on people,
the community in which it exists, and the larger world in which it operates is defined as
_____.

LANGUAGE SKILLS PRACTICE: PART 1 (CHAPTERS 1–4)

Proofread the following sentences. In the space provided, rewrite the sentences correctly. If you need to review English usage rules, check the Reference Section, pp. 583–599, in your text. Submit your work to your instructor.

DIRECTIONS: The following sentences contain errors in abbreviations; make the necessary corrections.

1. Elizabeth H. Crowther, Doctor of Philosophy, is teaching an organizational behavior course during the spring semester.

   _____

   _____

2. Doctor Josef Landow, Mr. Harry Curns, and Mrs. Angelis Franz make up the law firm of Landow, Curns, and Franz.

   _____

   _____

DIRECTIONS: The following sentences contain errors in capitalization; correct the sentences.

3. Carl Sandburg is my favorite poet; he wrote these lines:

   Why did he write to her,
   "I can't live with you"?
   and why did she write to him,
   "I can't live without you"?
   for he went west, she went east,
   and they both lived.

   _____

   _____

   _____

   _____

   _____

   _____

4. He plans to take algebra in the Fall and Psychology in the spring.

   _____

5. Next semester Sharon and Carlos will enroll in ethics 212.

   _____

DIRECTIONS: The following sentences contain errors in number usage; correct the sentences.

6. Every visitor to Italy will want to see 3 of the wonders of the ancient world.

   _____

7. In the 21st century there will be major changes in the international economy.

   _____

DIRECTIONS: Select the correct word from those shown in parentheses.

8. The director will be away for (a, an) hour.

   _____

9. We will gladly (accept, except) your offer.

   _____

10. Net profit has dropped (accept, except) during 1994.

   _____

11. We will leave the house (about, at about) ten o'clock.

   _____

DIRECTIONS: The following sentences contain errors in plurals and possessives; make the necessary corrections.

12. Marcus, Monique, and Harlan were second, third, and fourth runner-ups in the extemporaneous speaking contest.

   _____

13. Fulton-Calkins book was published by South-Western Educational Publishing, an International Thomson Publishing Company.

DIRECTIONS: The following sentences are punctuated incorrectly; make the necessary corrections.

14. Does this price Ms. Holzback include both the building and equipment.

   _____

15. The professor spoke with authority that is she set down the rules and expected them to be observed.

   _____

16. Jan Mary and June attended the meeting today Mark and Todd attended the meeting yesterday.

   _____

17. The company has increased its volume of business by nearly 200 percent over the past year no small achievement in these times.

   _____

DIRECTIONS: The following sentences contain misspelled words; correct the spelling.

18. Niether Heather nor Kevin plans to attend the communications seminar.

   _____

19. Beginning this week, our office will be located at One Main Place.

   _____

DIRECTIONS: The following words have been divided incorrectly. Correct the word division and provide the rule you followed in dividing the word correctly.

20. i-tems_____
    Rule: _____

21. mon-ths_____
    Rule:_____

22. nece-ssary _____
    Rule: _____

OA5-2 (GOALS 2 AND 3)

DIRECTIONS: Assume that you have a temporary assignment in the Computer Infor-mation Systems Department of your company. The CIS staff provides technical support and computer training sessions for all company employees. Among other duties, the of-fice staff assistant is responsible for maintaining scheduling logs. One log is used to schedule employees for training sessions, and another log shows which training rooms are used for each day of the week.

On your student template disk, file OA05-2, is a format for entering all of the sched-uled courses for the next training period. Using the information provided below and the information on student template disk, file OA05-2, enter the course information on a database file. Submit your file to your instructor.

Course Schedule: November

Microcomputers and DOS, DATA 10, 8:30–12:30
November 2, 16, 20, J. Hobson
Room 21A

Advanced DOS and Software Utilities, DATA 12, 1:30–4:30
November 5, J. Hobson
November 16, S. Kraubics
Room 21A

Word Processing Applications, DATA 11, 8:30–12:30
November 5, 12, I. Welsh, Room 21A
November 9, 16, S. Kraubics, Room 21B

Spreadsheets, Level I, DATA 15, 8:30–12:30
November 4, 17, B. Serwinzt
November 21, J. Hobson
Room 21C

Spreadsheets, Level II, DATA 16, 1:30–4:30
November 17, I. Welsh
November 23, J. Hobson
Room 21C

Introduction to Presentation Software, DATA 20, 8:30–10:30
November 16, Room 21A, B. Serwinzt
November 23, Room 21C, B. Serwinzt

Creating Macros, DATA 22, 2:30–4:30
November 9, 16, I. Welsh
Room 21B

OA5-4 (GOALS 2 AND 3)

DIRECTIONS: Here is a rough-draft copy of an article for the company's newsletter. Key the copy, making the corrections as indicated, using graphics, and formatting the document in two columns. Make a backup of your data on a floppy disk. Print a final copy and submit it to your instructor.

Conference Highlights *] All caps*

by Paul Simmins

Add graphic

The *Century 21* Communication Network Conference held in Chicago last week would have caused even non-computer "nuts" to get excited. Billed as an innovative technology showcase, the conference unveiled networking systems, imaging capabilities and highly sophisticated personal information manager products.

Add heading underline DS before and after each heading → Imaging

Aldron, Inc., introduced its document imaging software, which is used to add faxed and scanned images into certain applications. The images can be stored, copied, manipulated, and distributed ~~by~~ *with* applications such as electronic mail or databases.

Heading → PIM

A new PIM from Lorenz ~~can~~ top*s* an outliner and database to cross-reference data stored in its calendar, phonebook, ~~outliner~~ #, and to-do-list modules. This software will be available in standalone and networked versions. If we were to install this software on our network, it would enable group scheduling and multiuser outlining features.

Networking Systems

I was intrigued with a networking system that ~~had~~ may be a possibility ~~potential installation~~ for our satellite centers. The system permits up to 35 users to share files, printers, and other peripheral equipment. The LAN does not require technical expertise for installation, since it connects easily to each PCs parallel port.

Teleconferencing

The latest in teleconferencing was previewed by KOVANET. Network users can participate in electronic conferences regardless of their location. Security can be assured ~~issues have been addressed~~, and a feature for notetaking is built in

add
graphic User Group Reminder

At next month's user group meeting, I will
provide additional information from the
conference. The main topic for the meeting,
however, will be how to more efficiently use
the local area network for sharing files.

Chapter 5 Supplemental Exercise

DIRECTIONS: The Personnel Department of People First International maintains a database of their employees. Information such as home address, social security number, health benefit plan, number of dependents, and other confidential data is kept on the file. Certain information on the database is accessible by other departments, however. The name of the employees, date of employment, their departments, and work phone numbers are readily available.

Hugh Minor, the vice president of Communications, can access the database to learn the date employees joined the firm. On the date of their first and fifth anniversary, Mr. Minor would like to begin sending a memorandum acknowledging the contribution each employee makes to the company. (Special luncheons are held to recognize employees with ten years of service and above.)

Using the database file entitled SE05a, key the memorandum on the next page from Hugh Minor in final format; send the memorandum (using the form on the student data template in file OA02-1b) to each employee who joined the company in 1995 (fifth anniversary) and 2000 (first anniversary). Mr. Minor is beginning with employees at the corporate headquarters; the database file includes only those employees.

Before issuing the memorandum, you need to make the following changes to the file:

Add two employees:

Ruth Billingsley, Communications Department, 10/95, phone 1-1500
Tokomoto Kamoda, Information Systems, 7/95, phone 1-9665

Make these changes:

Rosemary Lipstein's last name is misspelled.
Chuck McDowel joined the company in June, not July.
Daphne Newsome now works in the Communications Dept., phone 1-1510.

Subj. – ANNIVERSARY RECOGNITION

All of us as People First International want to express our thanks to you for helping to make our company one of the best in the industry. When you joined us (one/five) year(s) ago, you became a part of a winning team.

In the past year our job placements rose by 8 percent; but even more important, our profitability improved by 10 percent. Your continued commitment to providing a quality service to our customers has contributed to this outstanding performance.

It takes the entire team to make People First International the industry leader that it is today. However, the team can be no greater than each of its capable and dedicated employees. YOU make our team what it is. Congratulations on your (first/fifth) anniversary with us. We look forward to celebration many successes together!

DIRECTIONS: Describe what is wrong with this picture, using what you have learned about ergonomics. Place your answers in the space provided below the picture. When you complete your answers, check them by referring to your student template disk in file OA06-4.

WHAT'S WRONG WITH THIS PICTURE?

_____   _____
_____   _____
_____   _____
_____   _____
_____   _____
_____   _____
_____   _____
_____   _____
_____   _____

OA6-5 (GOAL 5)

DIRECTIONS: Below is a draft of an announcement about a physical fitness program your company is beginning. The announcement will be distributed to all employees. Prepare a flyer to be printed on half sheets of paper (8½″ × 5½″). Make the flyer attractive and professional by using font enhancements, a border, and graphics. Print a copy and submit it to your instructor.

Join Our Physical Fitness Program Now!

Beginning Monday October 5, at 4:30 p.m. in Room 335, the first session of Physical Fitness will be held. We will meet three afternoons per week for one hour—Monday, Wednesday, and Friday afternoon.

Our first session will be a get acquainted one, with discussion centering on how future sessions will be conducted. Each session, after the initial one, will include forty minutes of aerobic exercise and twenty minutes of information concerning proper diet and relaxation techniques.

The sessions are free. Recognition will be given to those individuals who join and complete the program. Bring a coworker with you and join us on Monday.

DIRECTIONS: Below is a handwritten memo from the director of the Information Systems Department. Key the memorandum, using the form provided on the student template disk in file OA02-1b. Make the necessary corrections. Print a copy of it and submit it to your instructor.

TO: All Employees
FROM: Cary Alcevedos, Director
DATE: (put current date)
SUBJECT: COMPUTER VIRUS PROTECTION

We have been notified that some computer viruses have been reported in the area recently. Many computer users transfer ~~take~~ files to and from their office and home equipment. For this reason, it is essential that you provide protection for all of your computer sites.

Personal computers were infected last month with two viruses. The "Stoned-B/New Zealand #2" virus and the "Michaelangelo" virus attacked the boot sector of a personal computer, making the computer inoperable. Transfering files from one computer to another allowed the viruses to spread.

Viruses of this kind have the potential to destroy data on a hard disk drive.

In response to this situation, we have upgraded our virus protection software to detect and destroy these and over 2,000 other viruses. You should use the detection software immediately on all diskettes in both office and home computers to ensure they are virus free.

Please call me at 1-3352 if you have any questions or need assistance in using the virus protection software.

Contact the IS Department to obtain the detection software.

Chapter 6 Supplemental Exercise

DIRECTIONS: The Computer Information Systems Department conducted a company-wide survey to determine the need for or interest in certain applications software. Employees were asked to indicate the software they currently use in their jobs and the software they would like to use if purchased by the company. Software purchases and development of new training sessions are in part based on survey results. A summary of the responses is provided below. Create a bar graph to illustrate the data. Submit your bar graph to your instructor.

Software	Employees Use Currently	Employees Would Use if Purchased
Office Suites	212	16
Graphics as a standalone	44	26
Presentations as a standalone	100	150
Personal Informationt Management	134	108
Spreadsheets as a standalone	76	23

OA7-5 (GOAL 5)

DIRECTIONS: A section on printing services for an office procedures manual has been drafted. Part of the text appears on your template disk, file OA07-5. Revisions and additions to the text are provided below and on the following pages. Key the document, making the necessary changes. Print a copy for your instructor.

Printing Services (Center in all caps)

Overview

The company provides various methods for the production of printed materials. Some *regional and district* offices have small, low-volume copiers; the corporate office has a centrally located mid-volume copier. The most cost effective means of photocopying printed material exists in the company's central print shop. *(Insert A)*

Procedures

Employees wishing to have documents/projects printed must complete a Printing Requisition (Form 33). The project will be evaluated with the specifications given and a determination will be made by the printing technician if the job should be completed by the company's print shop or by an outside vendor. *(Insert B)*

(Insert C) Criteria for selecting the method of printing are paper size, paper weight, quantity, ink color, and special finishing requirements. Generally, the budget, or cost, of a project is a major consideration. In order to assist your planning for printing requests, a list of services and fees *for the central print shop* is provided in this section. ~~Prices for the central print shop are provided.~~ *on the accompanying chart*

The standard turnaround time needed for a simple reproduction job to be completed in-~~house~~ *of the central print shop* is two (2) days upon receipt ~~in~~ *of* the ~~print shop~~ *job.* However, if special paper needs to be ordered or if binding, three-hole punching, or any other finishing techniques required, time will be added as needed. The person originating the order will always be notified of the time extension needed to complete the job.

(Insert D)

1 1/2" L margin

SS document w/DS between paragraphs

2nd
Draft

Insert A Not only is the cost of reproducing material cheaper in a high-volume environment, but the savings in personal time spent is perhaps even more valuable.

(B) Whenever possible, the printing will be handled in-house, since this method is the most cost-effective.

(C) Services and Fees

The central print shop has limitations, however, based on equipment.

(D) If a request is received for a job that will be printed by an outside vendor, the average time required is seven to ten (7-10) working days. Some more complex jobs, however, will require a longer turnaround time

Understandably, the printing method ultimately dictates the length of time required for completion of a project. As you initiate printing requests, please take into account these considerations.

All Caps Bold

Print Shop Services and Fees

Includes this table at the end of the section

Service	Fee
Collating	NIC
Collating Folded Sheets (per 100 sheets)	$1.00
Folding (per fold for 100 sheets)	.30
Minimum charge	3.00
Stapling (upper left or side saddle per staple)	.01
Drilling (per hole for 100 sheets)	.02
Minimum charge	2.00
Trim (per 100 cuts)	.10
Padding (per pad up to 8 1/2" x 11")	.08
Minimum charge	1.00
Color Slip Sheets (per 100 sheets)	
8 1/2" x 11"	.95
8 1/2" x 14"	1.22
11" x 17"	1.90

Chapter 7 Supplemental Exercise

DIRECTIONS: Read the case below. In the space provided, respond to the items at the end of the case. Submit your responses to your instructor.

Central Retreat Hospital has been cited as one of the most expensive hospitals in the area based on patient stays. The total expenses of a patient's care include administrative as well as medical costs. The hospital's chief financial officer has charged managers with reducing their operating budgets by 5 percent for next year.

Ann Marie Nance manages the hospital's central printing center. In the past two years, she has noticed that the number of copies charged to departments throughout the hospital from the central print center has slowly decreased. The overall costs for copying at the hospital, however, have increased.

Ann Marie knows that many departments have purchased small, low-volume copiers. For example, the admissions department has a small console copier that is positioned in the hallway between the admissions office and the intake area for patients. It does not have a copy control device such as an access coding system. The maintenance department recently purchased a small tabletop copier; the service contract on the copier for one year is extremely high.

- Provide an analysis of the factors that may be leading to increased copying costs.

_____

_____

_____

_____

_____

_____

_____

_____

- Give several recommendations regarding copying that may be implemented to achieve the 5 percent reduction in operating costs.

_____

_____

_____

_____

_____

_____

Chapter 8 Supplemental Exercise

DIRECTIONS: Using the Internet or your local library, research the number of people who are working in virtual environments in your city and in the nation. Include those people who are working full time at home and those who are telecommuting either full or part time.

Prepare a graph of the statistics, showing the number of people in each area (virtual home environments, telecommuting full and part time) in your city compared to the same areas in the nation. Submit your report to your instructor.

VOCABULARY REVIEW: PART 2 (CHAPTERS 5–8)

DIRECTIONS: Complete the sentences below by supplying the correct word(s). Submit a copy to your instructor.

1. A device that can read keyboarded information and handwritten documents is called
   _____.

2. A device on a software package that uses a drop-down menu and various icons for executing commands and choosing program options is called _____.

3. A single miniature chip that contains the circuitry and components for arithmetic, logic, and control operations is called _____.

4. The brain of the computer system is the _____.

5. Networks that link various types of technological equipment within a building or several buildings within the same geographic area such as a business or a college campus are called _____.

6. A small, hand-controlled device that operates like a remote control box and allows the user to move the cursor and choose menu commands without using the keyboard is called
   _____.

7. The largest computer that accommodates hundreds of users doing different tasks is called
   _____.

8. The part of a computer that performs all the mathematical calculations is called _____
   _____.

9. A program that helps you store and manipulate data in a manner that allows fast and easy access is called _____.

10. Attempting to find solutions to hardware and software problems is called _____
    _____.

11. The two major categories of software programs are _____ and _____.

12. Programs that are sold with a computer as part of a combined hardware/software package are called _____.

13. A grid of rows and columns in which you enter numbers and text is called _____
    _____.

14. To help you eliminate stress when keyboarding over long periods of time, engage in
    _____ exercises.

15. A computer program that has unauthorized instructions that were introduced without permission or knowledge of the computer user has _____.

16. The process of making copies of documents is called _____.

17. A copy center that serves the large-volume copying needs of an organization is called

    _____.

18. A machine that cuts paper into strips or confetti-like material is called _____.

19. A type of copier that electronically sends an original document from one location to another via communication networks is called _____.

20. A person who knows what needs to be done and is anxious to get it done is called _____

    _____.

21. The smallest computer is called _____.

22. A recent development in monitors is the _____.

23. The operating system of a computer is referred as _____.

24. A statement written to clarify personal or organizational goals is called _____.

25. A US health care program that reimburses hospitals and physicians for care of individuals needing financial assistance is _____.

LANGUAGE SKILLS PRACTICE: PART 2 (CHAPTERS 5–8)

Proofread the following sentences. In the space provided, rewrite the sentences correctly. If you need to review English usage rules, check the Reference Section, pp. 583–599, in your text.

DIRECTIONS: The following sentences contain errors in number usage; correct the sentences.

1. The memorandum was dated April 8th; however, it did not reach the address until the twelfth of May

   _____

2. 80 people will attend the seminar.

   _____

3. The address of the company is forty-nine North Hopkins Street.

   _____

4. It will cost two thousand dollars to paint the office.

   _____

DIRECTIONS: Select the correct word from those shown in parentheses.

5. Randall left the office (sometime, some time) ago.

   _____

6. The office is a mile (farther, further) down the highway.

   _____

7. (Sometime, Some time) today I will complete the project.

   _____

8. Engineers will soon (advise, advice) the company which design should be used.

   _____

9. Please let me know when you checked (all of, all) the papers.

   _____

10. It is (alright, all right) for her to attend with you.

   _____

DIRECTIONS: The following sentences contain errors in plurals and possessives; make the necessary corrections.

11. This reference book is your's.

   _____

12. The receptionist desk was extremely cluttered.

_____

13. The Edward's women will attend the book signing.

_____

DIRECTIONS: The following sentences are punctuated incorrectly; make the necessary corrections.

14. The company has increased its volume of business by nearly 200 percent over the past year no small achievement in these times.

_____

15. He said "The first thing to do is to acquire the habit of studying the facts" she agreed with him.

_____

16. The presentation that she gave was a completely new one not the one I had heard her give previously.

_____

17. I believe Mary that you will agree with me.

_____

DIRECTIONS: The following sentences contain misspelled words; correct the spelling.

18. Most of his liesure time is spend at his cabin on Lake Chesdin.

_____

19. In the excitment of the moment, I failed to tell her about the call.

_____

DIRECTIONS: The following words have been divided incorrectly. Correct the word division and provide the rule you followed in dividing the word correctly.

20. is-n't _____

    Rule: _____

21. lis-ten _____

    Rule: _____

22. ground-ed _____

    Rule: _____

23. He'll _____

    Rule: _____

24. reg-ulate _____

    Rule: _____

25. self-con-trol _____

    Rule: _____

OA9-3 (GOALS 3 AND 4)

DIRECTIONS: Complete Item 1 below based on your perceptions of your own nonverbal behavior. Complete Item 2 by observing the nonverbal behavior of several people for three days in the school cafeteria, student lounge, your place of work, your home, or other places that you frequent. Compare your answers with one of your classmates. Discuss the differences and similarities between how you behave nonverbally and how your classmate and others behave nonverbally. Submit your completed form to your instructor.

NONVERBAL BEHAVIOR

1. List at least eight types of nonverbal behavior by which you reveal who you are, and describe a specific situation in which you use this behavior.

Nonverbal Behavior	Situation
_____	_____
_____	_____
_____	_____
_____	_____
_____	_____
_____	_____
_____	_____

2. Observe the nonverbal behavior of several people for three days (it does not need to be the same people each day) in the school cafeteria, student lounge, your place of work, your home, or other places that you frequent. Record the nonverbal behavior and your interpretation of the behavior on this form.

PERSON A

Nonverbal Behavior Observed	Interpretation of Behavior
_____	_____
_____	_____
_____	_____
_____	_____
_____	_____

PERSON B

Nonverbal Behavior Observed   Interpretation of Behavior

_____   _____
_____   _____
_____   _____
_____   _____
_____   _____
_____   _____

PERSON C

Nonverbal Behavior Observed   Interpretation of Behavior

_____   _____
_____   _____
_____   _____
_____   _____
_____   _____
_____   _____

PERSON D

Nonverbal Behavior Observed   Interpretation of Behavior

_____   _____
_____   _____
_____   _____
_____   _____
_____   _____
_____   _____

Chapter 9 Supplemental Exercise

DIRECTIONS: Analyze the letter below. Describe the tone of the letter. Make a list of the words and phrases that affect the message in a negative or positive manner. Rewrite the letter in a more positive tone, using the letterhead given on the student template disk, SE9. Submit your work to your instructor.

Letter

Mr. Emmett Alverez
XYZ Corporation
2358 Avenue G
Detroit, MI 4892 1-1879

Dear Mr. Alverez:

We are in receipt of your letter of complaint. You claim that the part-time employee who you hired from our firm is not competent. We cannot be responsible for every one of our employees. It is your responsibility to interview the person and determine whether or not the individual can fulfill the job duties of the position within your company.

Also, I would suggest that you might have trained the person for the specific work that you have. We cannot anticipate every company's needs. We do give our part-time people training, but when we do not know what you need, we cannot train for it.

Next time you call us for an employee, make certain that you clearly identify your needs so that we may work with you more closely.

Sincerely,

OA10-4 (GOALS 1, 2, AND 3)

DIRECTIONS: Refer to your textbook, p. 267, for the directions for this project, which is a collaborative writing one. Once the project is completed, you are to determine if your team worked collaboratively by using the project team evaluation form given here. Submit your evaluation form, along with the team report, to your instructor.

COLLABORATIVE WRITING PROJECT TEAM EVALUATION

As team members, evaluate the team by asking these questions and placing your answers in the space provided on the form:

- Did you determine the purpose of the writing assignment?

_____

- Did you determine who your audience was?

_____

- Did you select a team leader?

_____

- Did you set a work schedule?

_____

- Did you allocate the work by defining the tasks of each team member?

_____

OA10-4 (GOALS 1, 2, AND 3)

• How did you work together as a team? If you had conflicts, did you listen to each other, pay attention to cultural differences, and acknowledge each other's worth?

_____

_____

_____

_____

_____

_____

_____

_____

_____

_____

CHAPTER 10 SUPPLEMENTAL EXERCISE

DIRECTIONS: You have written a report on "Preparing Office Manuals." It has been edited by one of your teammates. The edited copy appears here. Prepare the report in final form, making all changes. You discover that there are also some misspelled words that the editor did not catch. Correct these spelling errors. Submit your report to your instructor.

Preparing Office Manuals — *Center Heading*

Office manuals are formal communications of objectives *management's* developed *that are developed* to acquaint employees with the policies and practices of a company. They are also used to assign *Certain duties and to establish procedures for* responsibility for performing those duties. A well written office manual saves time for both management and the employee. Office manuals should be written in a readable style, prepared economically, and distributed to each employee. *(Insert a)*

Types of Manuals *underline*

There are four types of office manuals commonly found; they are:

1. Policy Manual. This manual contains decisions, resolutions, and pronouncements off company policies established by the board of directors.

2. Organization Manual. This manual provides an explanation of the organization and responsibilities off various departments.

(Insert B) →

3. Departmental Practice Manual. This manual contains procedures for a particular department dealing with the internal policies, organization, and work methods of that department.

The type of manuals prepared and used within a company depends on the size of the company and whether the company's branches are decentralized or centralized. *the number of department in the company, the work performed in each department, and the centralization or decentralization of the company.*

General Information in Office Manuals

Office manuals are not uniformly organized. There are, however, certain ~~is~~ information pertaining to personnel policy ~~les~~ that should be present on all office manuals. They should include some statement as to how employees are hired, the difference between part-time and full-time employment, information about ~~merit rating~~ *performance evaluations,* and salary increases, as well as other general personnel information. For the sake off simplicity, a discussion of this information is presented in alphabetic order.

Insert C

Accidents. There should be more explanation of the workers' compensation law if the company is protected by such a law. Employees should be instructed to report immediately any personal accidents while working, even though the accident may seem trivial at first.

Change of address. Employees should be told that the personnel department *each* keeps a record of the names, home address, and telephone number of employees. In case of change, the personnel department should be notified immediately.

Move to after Accidents

Attendance. Employees should be told the importance of regular attendance and punctuality. If the company keeps a record of attendance and punctuality to be used in evaluating employees for promotions, employees should be so informed.

Insert E — *are to be reminded*

Insert D

Education. ~~Remind~~ employees that detailed information about ~~the~~ *their* educational ~~al~~ experiences is kept on file and used as a basis for advancement and promotion. If the company has a plan for paying part of all the tuition of employees who wish to further their education, the plan should be explained. Employees should ~~certainly~~ be *their* to discuss further educational possibilities with ~~his or her~~ immediate supervisor.

Insert S1

<u>Performance evaluations</u>. Employees should be told of periodic evaluations that are done by supervisors, ^ *and by the personnel department.*

<u>Probationary periods</u>. If the company assumes that employees are placed on probation for a period of ~~one~~ *three* to six months, it should be explained.

<u>Personal mail</u>. The attitude of the company toward employees receiving personal mail at the company address should be explained.

<u>Salary</u>. Employees should be told when and how they will be paid. Policies regarding salary increases should also be explained, along with the importance of keeping salary matters confidential.

Insert #2

<u>Telephone</u>.   An explanation of making and receiving personal telephone calls while at work should be given.

<u>Vacations</u>. Vacation policies should be explained for both full-time and part-time employees.

One of the *greatest* difficulties in preparing office manuals for new employees is obtaining agreement from company executives on what practices and policies should be included. The development of the manual is usually initiated and supervised by the office in charge of that department if only departmental manuals are involved. If more elaborate manuals are planned, one person should probably assume complete charge in planning them, outlining procedures for preparation, editing, publishing, *ing* distribution, and revising manuals. Whatever the format, office manuals should be prepared so that material can be easily inserted.

Insert #1

(Insert A) It provides valuable information in printed form and eliminates the need for repetitious instructions.

(Insert B) 3. Administrative Practice Manual. Standard procedures and methods for performing the company's work are given in this manual.

(Insert C) Absence. This section of an office manual should state clearly company policies regarding absences of employees. It should explain whether employees are paid for absences and to whom they should report in case of absence.

(Insert D) Credit union. If the company has a credit union for the convenience of employees, detailed information about participation should be made available.

(Insert E) Each employee should be reminded that previous education plays a prominent part in selecting a person for a particular job.

(Insert F1)

Hospitalization. If the company has a plan where employees can take advantage of the services offered by a medical service organization, the plan should be explained.

put in alpha order

Group Insurance. If the company has an insurance plan for employees, the plan should be outlined, or the employees should be told that detailed information will be provided at a certain time.

(Insert G)

A well-organized office manual can prove to be an invaluable aid for employees.

(Insert F2)

Special Needs. Employees with disabilities that require special needs should be notified of the company's obligations to meet their needs.

DIRECTIONS: Key the handwritten letter below; use the letterhead on the Student Template Disk in file OA11-1. Correct any errors that are in the letter and use the appropriate format. Submit your work to your instructor.

Mr. Bruce Cloninger
Placement Representative
Computer Institute
901 West Franklin Street
Detroit MI

Dear Bruce;

People First International has a need for individuals who are interested in a computer career. The Computer Development Program is an intensive two-year training program that provides the industry knowledge and technical expertise needed for success in our environment. Candidates must have a degree in business, with specialization in computers, an above-average grade point average, a track record of leadership ability, and a willingness to relocate within the United State or to international sites in France and Germany.

The long-term growth picture for People First International is excellent. We expect to employ fifty new employees this year. We anticipate maintaining this level of staffing in the future.

Enclosed for your information are the following materials—Computer Development Program Description, People First International Employee Guide, benefit summary, and a brochure entitled, Success in Business with People First International.

I welcome the opportunity to talk further with interested students. If you have any questions regarding People First International please contact me.

Sincerely,

Kyle Kronan
Corporate Recruiter

CHAPTER 11 SUPPLEMENTAL EXERCISE

DIRECTIONS: Mr. Menendez recently was asked to serve on the program committee that coordinates the planning of an annual conference on global economic development. He composed a draft of the letter on his computer to be sent to four individuals, inviting them to speak at the conference. The topic is "Latin-American Trade Practices and Opportunities." The letter is on the student template disk in file SE11a. The letter must be formatted and all errors corrected. The letter is to be sent to the individuals listed below. Use the letterhead provided on the student template disk in files SE11(2)–(5). Submit your work to your instructor.

- Dr. K. A. Lepzinski
  Kirchhoff Consultants
  906 Lake Drive
  Royal Oak, MI 48068

- Mr. Arthur B. Mullennix
  Melching, Inc.
  2110 Fuller
  Southfield, MI 48075

- Ms. Alana Steeby
  The Gerritt Company
  1370 Buttrick SE
  Detroit, MI 48142

- Mr. John Vrona
  Bertsch Company
  6906 Riverview Drive
  Detroit, MI 48201

OA12-3 (GOAL 3)

DIRECTIONS: Each of the messages on the five telephone message pads given here is incomplete. Supply the answers to the questions provided on the following page; correct the telephone message pads. Submit your work to your instructor.

1.

To ___Claude Peterson___
Date ___4/16___ Time ___2:10___ A.M. ☐ P.M. ☑

WHILE YOU WERE OUT
M ___Wendall Beale___
of ___Shreveport LA___
Phone _____555-1205_____
    Area Code   Number   Extension

TELEPHONED	☒	PLEASE CALL	☒
CALLED TO SEE YOU		WILL CALL AGAIN	
WANTS TO SEE YOU		**URGENT**	☒
RETURNED YOUR CALL			

Message ___Needs a cost estimate ASAP___

___ASJ___
Operator

2.

To ___Janice Bobb___
Date ___4/16___ Time ___2:36___ A.M. ☐ P.M. ☑

WHILE YOU WERE OUT
M ___C. J. McDonald___
of ___Wynn, Inc. North Platte___
Phone ___308- 555-9600___
    Area Code   Number   Extension

TELEPHONED	☒	PLEASE CALL	☒
CALLED TO SEE YOU		WILL CALL AGAIN	
WANTS TO SEE YOU		**URGENT**	
RETURNED YOUR CALL			

Message _____

___ASJ___
Operator

3.

To ___Gene Hansborough___
Date ___4/16___ Time ___2:45___ A.M. ☐ P.M. ☑

WHILE YOU WERE OUT
M ___Professor Akers___
of ___Princeton University___
Phone _____555-1705_____
    Area Code   Number   Extension

TELEPHONED	☒	PLEASE CALL	☒
CALLED TO SEE YOU		WILL CALL AGAIN	
WANTS TO SEE YOU		**URGENT**	
RETURNED YOUR CALL			

Message _____

___ASJ___
Operator

4.

To ___Stan Lamuir___
Date ___4/16___ Time ___2:53___ A.M. ☐ P.M. ☑

WHILE YOU WERE OUT
M ___David___
of ___Boston___
Phone ___FAX   555-7207___
    Area Code   Number   Extension

TELEPHONED	☒	PLEASE CALL	
CALLED TO SEE YOU		WILL CALL AGAIN	
WANTS TO SEE YOU		**URGENT**	
RETURNED YOUR CALL			

Message ___Fax the 1st qtr. Sales figures to arrive in the office by noon tomorrow___

___ASJ___
Operator

5.

```
┌─────────────────────────────────────┐
│  To ___Francis Bernstein_____  │
│                                       │
│  Date __4/16_____ Time __3:10__     │
│                              A.M. ☐   │
│                              P.M. ☑   │
│                                       │
│       WHILE YOU WERE OUT              │
│  M _Mike Grassick_____   │
│                                       │
│  of _____  │
│                                       │
│  Phone _____   │
│       Area Code   Number   Extension  │
│  ┌──────────────────┬──────────────┐  │
│  │ TELEPHONED       │ PLEASE CALL ⊠│  │
│  ├──────────────────┼──────────────┤  │
│  │ CALLED TO SEE YOU│ WILL CALL    │  │
│  │                  │ AGAIN        │  │
│  ├──────────────────┼──────────────┤  │
│  │ WANTS TO SEE YOU │              │  │
│  ├──────────────────┤ URGENT       │  │
│  │ RETURNED YOUR CALL│             │  │
│  └──────────────────┴──────────────┘  │
│                                       │
│  Message ___Staying at the_____   │
│  ___Ritz-Carlton in Paris_____   │
│  _____  │
│  ___Call tomorrow if possible_____   │
│  _____  │
│  _____ASJ_____   │
│              Operator                 │
└─────────────────────────────────────┘
```

Message 1: What is the area code for Shreveport? _318_____

_____

Message 2: In which state is North Platte? _NE_____

Message 3: Where is Princeton University located, and what is the area code? _NJ - 609_____

_____

Message 4: What is the latest by our time (Detroit, Michigan) that we must fax the sales figures to arrive in the

Atlanta office tomorrow by noon? _____

_____

Message 5: What is the international directory assistance number to call in order to get the number of the

Ritz-Carlton in Paris? ____00_____

OA12-5 (GOALS 3 AND 4)

DIRECTIONS: Mr. Menendez is on the Northwest Savings Bank Board and is on a sub-committee that is charged with improving banking services. Mr. Menendez has asked you to help him with this project, which is the design of a survey form. Here is some background information that may be helpful for you.

The Board committee, along with Leon Pavilottus who is vice president of customer service, is seeking several long-term customers to be "shoppers" for various onsite and telephone services provided by the bank. The shoppers conduct normal business transactions and provide an evaluation of the service they received. The customers who serve as shoppers do so anonymously—in other words, the bank's employees do not know which customers are "shoppers."

Design a survey form to be used by the shoppers based on the information given here. Submit your survey form to your instructor.

Information for form:

Title: Telephone Service Evaluation form
Date and time of call
Branch office and department called
Blanks for yes or no for the following questions:
   Was the call answered promptly (within 3 rings)?
   Was the call placed on hold?
      If yes, was permission asked before placing the call on hold?
   Was the call transferred to another extension?
      If yes, was the transfer handled properly?
      In no, please explain
   Was the caller's name used during the transaction?
   Were questions answered completely and courteously?
      If no, please explain

With how many employees did the caller have to speak before completing the
purpose of the call?

    Please circle 1   2   3   4   Other

Overall Rating: Excellent___ Very Good___ Good___ Poor___

Comments:

Chapter 12 Supplemental Exercise

DIRECTIONS: You are working for Mr. Juan Menendez. You receive the following telephone calls. Write a brief script of how you would respond to each caller. Submit the situations, along with a copy of your script for each situation to your instructor.

1. Bobbi Albright calls to speak with Mr. Menendez; you think that Ms. Albright is in sales for Heminway Corporation, but you cannot remember for certain. Mr. Menendez is in his office, but he has told you that he does not want to take any calls from sales representatives.

2. A person calls, sounding somewhat agitated, and asks to speak with "the person in charge," but he will not give you his name or the purpose of his call.

3. Roger Shields, a major client, calls for Mr. Menendez. Your company recently provided several employees for Mr. Shields. Mr. Shields has complained about the lack of training of these employees. Mr. Menendez is not in when Mr. Shields calls. When you tell Mr. Shields that he is not in the office, he starts yelling at you about how incompetent and inept your company is.

4. Ms. Holly Arlston has an appointment with Mr. Menendez at 2 p.m. She calls at 1:50 p.m. from her cellular phone; a traffic accident will cause her to be at least 45 minutes late. Ms. Arlston wants to know if she can meet with Mr. Menendez at 3 p.m. Mr. Menendez mentioned to you this morning that he would like to leave today by 3 p.m. since it is his wife's birthday. He is on a long-distance telephone call, and you cannot ask him if he is willing to stay.

DIRECTIONS: The following two letters were received in the morning mail. Annotate these letters and submit them to your instructor.

5456 Hammock ■ Detroit, MI 48242-3478 ■ Phone: 313 555-1934 Fax: 313 555-2034

March 10, 2000

Mr. Juan Menendez
People First, International
986 Front Street
Detroit, MI 48201-1701

Dear Mr. Menendez:

Thank you for the opportunity to review your mailroom concerns in our meeting last week. From the information you provided me, our staff believes your company can become more cost-effective by updating your equipment, adding several software packages, and training your mailroom personnel on both the equipment and software packages.

Our company is prepared to provide the expertise necessary to assist you in making these changes. We will need to spend approximately one week on-site at People First. From that point, we will recommend the appropriate equipment and software packages. We will then spend approximately one additional week training your personnel, once the equipment and software are received. We will provide you with two of our highly knowledgeable personnel for the two weeks; the total cost for the two weeks of staff time, plus the proposal recommending the equipment and software necessary, will be $8,000. You will be able to offset the $8,000 quickly due to productivity increases with the proposed equipment and software. In fact, I suggest that the entire project, considering both the costs of the equipment and software, will be offset within one year due to increased efficiency of employees and a reduction in the costs of mailing and shipping services.

I look forward to hearing from you soon as to your decision. We will be able to send in out staff immediately once we hear from you.

Sincerely,

Roger Vanderlaan

Roger Vanderlaan
Vice President

LONGWOOD CORPORATION

◆◆◆

825 Dorchester Avenue ◊ ◊   ◊ ◊   ◊ ◊   ◊ ◊ Detroit, MI 48100-3402

March 14, 2000

Mr. Juan Menendez
People First, International
986 Front Street
Detroit, MI 48201-1701

Dear Mr. Menendez:

Our company is interested in working with you in providing part-time office assistance
in our offices in Germany and France. As I explained to you when we talked, we are
planning an expansion in both countries. We will need to add approximately 20 office
personnel within the next year.

We found your proposal detailing the services that you can provide most acceptable. I
am enclosing a signed copy of this proposal. I would like to set up a time to talk with
you sometime next week about the details of our needs. I look forward to hearing from
you with a date and time.

Sincerely,

Rebecca Ragstein

Rebecca Ragstein
Vice President of International Operations

Enclosure

(Note to student: Mr. Menendez will be in France all next week.)

Chapter 13 Supplemental Exercise

DIRECTIONS: Your employer is serving as Chairman of the Board of the local Chamber of Commerce. The Chamber is planning their annual economic development conference. Your employer will be working closely with the Steering Committee for this conference. He has given you a list of their names that you have placed on a mailing list. However, there have been some changes to the committee. Retrieve the database file (file SE13) on the student template disk. Make the changes given here.

Montague Trading: Shantee Williams, Vice President
Klassen T. Industries: M. M. Nissen, CEO
The DuMundie Group: Robert Mosely, CEO

Sort the file by ZIP code for a mailing; run a copy of the database; print out the mailing labels. Submit your database copy and the mailing labels to your instructor.

VOCABULARY REVIEW: PART 3 (CHAPTERS 9–13)

DIRECTIONS: Complete the sentences below by supplying the correct word(s). Submit a copy to your instructor.

1. The ability to "make known; to impart; to transmit information, thought, or feeling so that it is adequately received and understood" is referred to as _____.

2. The way you see yourself—who you believe you are, what your strengths and weaknesses are, and how you believe others see you is referred to as _____.

3. The process of exchanging ideas and feelings through the use of words is called _____ _____.

4. The process of turning an idea into symbols that can be communicated is called _____ _____.

5. The act of laying claim to and defending a territory is termed _____.

6. When grammatically equivalent forms are used within a sentence, it is referred to as _____.

7. When the subject of the sentence receives the action or is acted upon, it is referred to as _____.

8. The Gunning Fog Index and Flesch-Kincaid Index are _____.

9. This symbol, ⟩G⟨, and other similar symbols when writing e mail, is called _____ _____.

10. The approach that requires the writer to place the reader at the center of the messages is called the _____.

11. The two basic letter styles used today are _____.

12. The two punctuation styles used today are _____.

13. The process of giving credit to the sources used in a report is called _____.

14. Comparing two different things by stressing the similarities between the two is called using _____.

15. The fastest mail service available from USPS is _____.

16. The class of mail that includes letters, greeting cards, and postcards is _____.

17. A mail service that provides maximum protection and security for valuable items is

    _____.

18. The communication of text, data, images, or voice messages between a sender and recipient by utilizing telecommunications links is _____.

19. Underlining important points in a piece of correspondence or writing notes in the margin of the correspondence is called _____.

20. Two automated pieces of equipment used by USPS to scan and sort mail are _____ and _____.

21. The electronic transmission of text, data, voice, video, and/or graphics is called _____

    _____.

22. A network that links various types of equipment used within a building or several buildings within the same geographic area is called _____.

23. A service provided by the local phone company that offers PBX-like features to a business without the business purchasing a switching system is called _____.

24. A service that integrates voice, e mail, and fax messaging is called _____.

25. A telephone service in which a subscriber pays a fixed charge for long-distance calls to a particular area is called _____.

LANGUAGE SKILLS PRACTICE: PART 3 (CHAPTERS 9–13)

Proofread the following sentences. In the space provided, rewrite the sentences correctly. If you need to review English usage rules, check the Reference Section, pp. 583–599, in your text. Submit your work to your instructor.

DIRECTIONS: The following sentences contain errors in abbreviations; make the necessary corrections.

1. The program starts at 8:45 A.M. on Wednesday, Mar. 25.

   _____

2. The building is located on Azalea Blvd.

   _____

3. The Hon. Susan Baynes Harris will speak at the meeting.

   _____

DIRECTIONS: The following sentences contain errors in capitalization; correct the sentences.

4. We have planned trips to the northeast and southwest this summer and fall.

   _____

5. She is an office assistant for the business division of Chesapeake Community college.

   _____

DIRECTIONS: The following sentences contain errors in number usage. Correct the sentences.

6. Her daughter is almost sixteen.

   _____

7. Approximately 20 people are in my class, and 15 of them were in my last class.

   _____

8. In military correspondence, dates are written in this manner: November 15, 2001.

   _____

DIRECTIONS: Select the correct word from those shown in parentheses.

9. There was a disagreement (between, among) the team's members.

_____

10. Pam feels (bad, badly) today.

_____

11. Everyone in the room knows that Austin is the (capital, capitol) of Texas.

_____

12. That is a (capital, capitol) idea!

_____

13. When the lawsuit is tried, our (council, counsel, consul) is planning to (cite, site) several recent court decisions.

_____

DIRECTIONS: The following sentences contains errors in plurals and possessives; make the necessary corrections.

14. The two secretaries raucous laughter disturbed the other employees in the office.

_____

15. The women's coats were checked in the lobby of the building.

_____

DIRECTIONS: The following sentences are punctuated incorrectly. Make the necessary changes.

16. People materials and production are three essential components of any organization.

_____

17. The salesperson said, Show the client how using the computer will save the company money.

_____

18. Fill in the form put it in the envelope it is stamped and addressed and mail it today.

_____

DIRECTIONS: The following sentences contain misspelled words. Correct the spelling.

19. Having traveled throughout Europe and the Middle East on numerous occasions, he was considered a world traveller.

   _____

20. Potatos are a common vegetable and can be used in a variety off dishes.

   _____

21. There are three attornies who have offices in this building.

   _____

DIRECTIONS: The following words have been divided incorrectly. In the space provided, show the correct word division and provide the rule you followed in dividing the word correctly.

22. self-satis-fied _____

   Rule: _____

23. grad-uation _____

   Rule: _____

OA14-2 (GOALS 1 AND 2)

DIRECTIONS: Correspondence from the clients listed below are to be placed in a numeric file. Assign numbers to the clients beginning with No. 100 for the first name on the list, with the next name assigned 101, and so forth. After the numbers are assigned, prepare 3 × 5 cards for the card file by listing the clients' names in indexing order and placing the appropriate number on the card. Arrange the cards in alphabetical order. Submit your cards to your instructor.

Grant's Drum City
Lee Gray and Company
Andy Grantella Tuneup
Grand Prairie Self Storage
Greentree Pharmacy
Green Tree Apartments
Greenfields, Inc.
Earl Greenlee Custom Drapery
Great American Coverup
Great China Restaurant
Greater Mount Olive Baptist Church
Green Bay Packaging
Guaranty Bank
Gulf American Products
Gulf Fire Sprinklers, Inc.
Jose Gutierrez
Jerry Gukoff
Gypsi Enterprises, Inc.
Gyo Ha Industrial Co.
Boyce Graham Photography
Ms. Marie M. Graham
Ms. Wilma Grainger
Grandbury State Bank
Grand Avenue Clinic
Grand Bancshares, Inc.
J. W. Grandstaff, Jr.
J. W. Grandstaff, Sr.
Grattafiori Corporation
Cecil Grattafiori, II
Cecil Grattafiori, III
Graveley Hardware
Graphic Finishers
Gray Maintenance Contractors
Veo Gray, Realtor
Tom Gray Paint Company
Gray's Diesel
Gray-Collin Electric
Gray's Nursery

OA14-3 (GOALS 1 AND 2)

DIRECTIONS: Add the names below to the database that you are creating in OA14-3, p. 393, of your text. Once you add the names to the database, print out a copy and submit it to your instructor.

Add these records:

Mountain Rafters, District, MI 48216

Outfetters, Inc., District, MI 48220

Italy Corporation, District, MI 48219

OA14-4 (GOALS 1 AND 2)

DIRECTIONS: In OA14-4, p. 393 of your text, you are to prepare a cross-reference sheet for the letter to MHOLMS. The cross-reference sheet form to be used is given below.

CROSS-REFERENCE SHEET

Name of Subject   File No.

Regarding   Date

SEE

Name or Subject   File No.

DIRECTIONS: This list of names is to be merged in alphabetical order with the names on the student template disk in the file OA14-5. Once the names have been merged, print a copy and submit it to your instructor.

The 4 Entertainers
Allen Erbs Plant Shop
Doctor Erb's Shop
East West Airport
Eighth Street Drug
FROX Radio Station
The Four Acres
T. E. Forfang
Roger R. Ford Credit
4 L Plumbing
11 Street Coiffures
Brother Ford
Eat More Burger Company
Down Town Merchants
Forty Cleaners
R. T. Frazier (ainesville)
Georgia E. Forde
El Tec Sales, Inc.
The Ely Company
Erma and Fay's Beauty Shop
E Z Cleaning Service
R. T. Frazier (Jacksonville)
Mrs. Foretich Chung
William T. Ford
Edsel O. Ford
Ann D. Ford
Andrew Ford, Sr.
A. F. Ford
A. J. Ford, Sr.
A. J. Ford, Jr.
Ernst and Ernst Accountants
Brother Ford's Candy Shop
DeKalb Jewelers
M. R. D'Fore
D G Motors
E and E Record Company
James Foree
Winetta ForeAft
Harriette W. Ford
Father Michael
DelNorte Lock Company

Chapter 14 Supplemental Exercise

DIRECTIONS: As part of its records retrieval procedures, the organization for which you work uses a printed requisition form for charging out records. It is a fairly expensive form to print, since it is printed in duplicate on NCR paper. The Records Department manager recommended that several routinely used forms be created as templates and put on the local area network.

Design a requisition form for charging out files that can be put on the system and easily accessed by all computer users. The form should be designed so that it can be printed on a half sheet of paper or on a 5.5 × 4.25 card.

Using the form you created, complete a requisition for each of the following situations in which files are being checked out.

1. Letter requested is from Del Norte Lock Company dated September 20 about servicing the vault; requested by Edward Robinson, Accounting, on October 1; to be returned by October 9.

2. Letter requested is from DeKalb Jewelers dated September 14 concerning price quotation; requested by Kathrine Malcolm, Accounting, on November 15; to be returned by November 18.

3. Report from Karla Mikimoto dated November 1 concerning reorganization; requested by Jada Bartlett, Human Resources, on November 29; to be returned by December 5.

4. Letter requested is from A. D. Ford concerning bankruptcy; requested by John Anders, Accounting; date of letter, November 24; letter requested on December 2; to be returned by December 10.

OA15-1 (GOAL 1)

DIRECTIONS: Karla Mikimoto, records manager, has made revisions to the records retention and disposition schedule to be submitted for review at this week's executive officers' meeting. The revisions are shown here. The original document appears on the student template disk, OA15.1. Use the strikethrough feature to show material to be deleted, and underline all new wording. This will aid the reviewers in understanding revisions to the document. Identify the document as Draft 2 and submit it to your instructor.

DRAFT

DRISCOLL & CLINE
Records Retention and Disposition Schedule

This schedule is continuing authority for the retention and disposition of the records as stated and supersedes previously approved applicable schedules.

Record Category/Title	Scheduled Retention and Disposition
1. Acknowledgment File	Destroy 3 months after acknowledgment and referral
Add 2. _Administrative Databases_ _See Electronic Records_	
3 ~~2~~. Administrative Files See Correspondence Records	
4 ~~3~~. Board/Conference/Committee Meeting Records	
a. Records ~~relating~~ _Pertaining_ to executive establishment, organization, membership, and policy	Retain 3 years for administrative use; purge all material of non-enduring value and/or microfilm according to standards
b. Records created by agenda, minutes, final reports, and related records documenting the accomplishment of official boards	_Same as 4a_ Retain ~~3 years for administrative use; purge all material of non-enduring value and/or microfilm according to standards~~

5 4. Correspondence Records

    a. Correspondence/subject files of executive officers not duplicateded elsewhere that document establishment of policies, procedures, and achievements

Same as 4a

Retain ~~3 years for administrative use; purge all material of non-enduring and/or microfilm according to standards~~

    b. ~~General correspondence:~~ Letters of inquiry, ~~informative or suggestive in nature~~, which address specific issues, projects, or cases or refer to corporate operations

Retain same as 4 a

    c. ~~Administrative files:~~ Inquiries, responses, letters and ~~&~~ other miscellaneous correspondence, generated in the course of daily business

Retain same as 4 a

8 5. Environmental Impact Files

Permanent

9 6. Publications
Pamphlets, reports, brochures, published or processed

Retain until superseded manuals, and other and then transfer 1 copy to the archive files

10 7. Reference Files

Review annually; remove and destroy all nonessential material

11 8. Records Management Documents ~~Records~~ Documents ~~Records~~ that relate to the management of records, including ~~such matters~~ forms, correspondence, reports, mail, and files management; the use of (d) microforms, work processing, vital records programs; and all other aspects of records management not covered elsewhere in this schedule

Permanent until superseded or revised

Add

6. Electronic Mail/FAX Documents | Retain with related files or records and follow established retention and disposition for that file or record

7. Electronic Records
   a. Created solely to test system performance, such as test records, as well as documentation for the electronic files/records | Delete/destroy when no longer needed

   b. Used to create or update a master file, including but not limited to, work files, valid transaction files, and intermediate input/output records | Delete after information has been transferred to the master file and verified

   c. Serve to replace, in whole or part, administrative records scheduled for disposable under one or more items in the General Schedule no longer needed, | Delete after the expiration of the retention period authorized for the disposable hard copy or when whichever is later

   d. Serve as administrative databases that support administrative functions | Destroy or delete when superseded or obsolete or upon authorized destruction of related master file or database

   e. Created as word processing files, such as letters, messages, memoranda, reports, policies, and manuals recorded on hard or floppy diskettes | Delete when no longer needed to create a hard copy

OA15-2 (GOAL 1)

DIRECTIONS: Karla Mikimoto has asked you to prepare a database that includes information about all employees in the Records and Information Systems Department. Each employee has completed a form listing a variety of personnel information. The completed forms are given below and on the following page. Create a database that includes the information from the forms. Print a copy of the database for your instructor.

EMPLOYEE INPUT FORM

Employee #	Last Name	First Name	MI
5512-5239	Okano	Hayato	K.

Address
1514 Wentworth Drive

City	State	Zip	OFFICE USE ONLY	
Detroit	MI	48202-1595		

Phone	Date Employed (YY/MM/DD)	Hourly Wage
555-459-2493	00/04/15	$8.75

Date of Birth (YY/MM/DD)	Sex	Job Title
75/02/24	M	File Clerk

Withholding Allowances	Marital Status	Department
3	M	Records Management

EMPLOYEE INPUT FORM

Employee #	Last Name	First Name	MI
3952-3948	Reynolds	Estelle	L.

Address
25369 Wenonah Street

City	State	Zip	OFFICE USE ONLY	
Detroit	MI	48201-2323		

Phone	Date Employed (YY/MM/DD)	Hourly Wage
555-456-1383	97/12/05	$10.25

Date of Birth (YY/MM/DD)	Sex	Job Title
73/05/06	F	File Clerk

Withholding Allowances	Marital Status	Department
1	S	Records Management

EMPLOYEE INPUT FORM

Employee #	Last Name	First Name	MI
1955-2452	Garcia	Michael	P.

Address
46202 Broad Bend Avenue

City	State	Zip	**OFFICE USE ONLY**	
Detroit	MI	48201-4203		

Phone		Date Employed (YY/MM/DD)	Hourly Wage
555-451-3304		91/10/13	$12.35

Date of Birth (YY/MM/DD)		Sex	Job Title
66/08/12		M	File Clerk

Withholding Allowances	Marital Status	Department
5	M	Records Management

EMPLOYEE INPUT FORM

Employee #	Last Name	First Name	MI
1735-7869	Johnson	Richard	J.

Address
6983 South Friendship Road

City	State	Zip	**OFFICE USE ONLY**	
Detroit	MI	48203-1937		

Phone		Date Employed (YY/MM/DD)	Hourly Wage
555-454-9043		97/06/13	$10.40

Date of Birth (YY/MM/DD)		Sex	Job Title
76/04/22		M	File Clerk

Withholding Allowances	Marital Status	Department
3	M	Records Management

EMPLOYEE INPUT FORM

Employee #	Last Name	First Name	MI
2319-3068	Hastings	Francise	G.

Address
6983 Sterling Parkway West, Apartment 16

City	State	Zip	**OFFICE USE ONLY**	
Detroit	MI	48223-4562		

Phone		Date Employed (YY/MM/DD)	Hourly Wage
555-459-2345		99/11/08	$9.65

Date of Birth (YY/MM/DD)		Sex	Job Title
73/03/01		F	File Clerk

Withholding Allowances	Marital Status	Department
3	S	Records Management

Chapter 15 Supplemental Exercise

DIRECTIONS: Below are copies of two directory files from your supervisor's hard disk. Loren VanPelt does not always save her files to the appropriate directory; thus, over a period of time her files get mixed together and she cannot readily retrieve documents. Loren saves all of her correspondence by an "L" or "M" prefix for letters and memos, and forms have a suffix of "FOR." She files her travel reports with the name "TRIP" or sometimes with the suffix "TRA."

   Review the printouts of these two directories. The recommendation is that Loren should establish four subdirectories—Correspondence, Forms, General, and Travel. Determine which files should be moved to each directory. Write the name of the directory by each file. Submit your work to your instructor.

12-05-01   Directory C:\My Documents*.*
Free: 23,078,554

.	Current		<DIR>		
ACCTG			4,951	03-29-00	04:40P
CPED			28,789	05-26-00	03:15P
ITIN	TRA		3,334	05-04-00	09:50A
L-JTFER	LVP		6,452	05-05-00	08:58A
L-GROVES			3,101	07-30-00	10:14A
L-RLCAR	LVP		8,775	05-09-00	02:45P
L-TRANSL			13,498	04-11-00	10:23A
M-ACCTG			9,678	07-13-00	02:30P
M-BUDGET	LVP		7,933	05-12-00	09:33A
M-EDPR			15,654	01-19-00	07:45A
M-PLAN			3,590	05-22-00	08:55A
M-SPACE			2,554	06-14-00	11:39A
M-VDOT			10,324	11-03-00	12:10P
M-WARNE			8,101	04-22-00	04:12P
STAPLES			7,437	06-12-00	12:05P
TRANSPO	TRA		7,221	06-06-00	11:45A
TRIP1	TEX		12,090	05-24-00	09:11A
TRIP2	COL		8,945	08-10-00	01:22P
TRIP3	ALA		9,987	10-05-00	02:50P
VAPERS			28,642	09-17-00	10:12A

12-05-01　　　　　　　　　　　　　Directory C:\My Documents/LVP/*.*
Free: 21,789,020

.	Current		<DIR>		
ANNE			9,459	04-15-00	08:28A
ANNEVAL			12,978	02-04-00	02:01P
ASTOR			3,907	06-08-00	05:15P
BIO-SHOR			5,087	07-28-00	08:29A
BIO43			10,312	07-30-00	10:39A
BUDGET	FOR		8,740	08-19-00	11:04A
D-PROP	SUM		6,398	05-12-00	01:46P
DIRECT			38,451	04-22-00	03:49P
EL-MINS			8,391	07-16-00	09:38A
JOBDESC			10,329	05-28-00	11:34A
FI-PROOF			3,290	02-12-00	08:37A
L-ATLEE			2,556	03-16-00	09:58A
L-PAPER			4,489	04-06-00	01:19P
LPTA			3,833	05-17-00	04:59P
L-RESUME			7,911	10-19-00	04:22P
L-SCHOL			10,047	11-21-00	07:59A
M-DSTRIP	LVP		2,558	05-12-00	09:59A
M-LEAVE			3,975	11-30-00	04:45P
M-PROMO			9,226	05-09-00	11:27A
MILEAGE	TRA		12,534	02-27-00	10:48A
PROOF	FOR		29,756	04-25-00	03:15P
ROD-BIO			6,799	06-11-00	09:14A
RCC	FOR		31,224	07-24-00	01:57P
SCH-CU			2,997	08-26-00	02:46P
TRAVEL	FOR		24,513	10-13-00	04:10P

VOCABULARY REVIEW: PART 4 (CHAPTERS 14–15)

DIRECTIONS: Complete the sentences below by supplying the correct word(s). Submit a copy to your instructor.

1. The systematic control of records over the record life cycle is referred to as _____.

2. The manner in which records are classified for storage is referred to as _____.

3. A method of storage in which records are filed by numbers is referred to as _____.

4. A filing method organized by the final digits of a term is called _____.

5. An arrangement of records in date order is referred to as _____.

6. The process of determining the name to be used in storing is called _____.

7. The process of marking the units of a filing segment by which the record is to be stored is called _____.

8. When a record is likely to be called for under two or more names, it should be _____ _____.

9. A form used to request a record to be borrowed is called _____.

10. Records that cannot be replaced and should never be destroyed are called _____ _____.

11. The process of continually transferring records from the active to the inactive files is called _____.

12. Records that are used three or four times a month are called _____.

13. Folders that hang from small metal rods attached to the folder are called _____.

14. Records that are necessary to an orderly continuation of the business and are replaceable only with considerable expenditure of time and money are known as _____.

15. The process of reviewing a record to see that it has been acted upon before placing it in a file is called _____.

16. A collection of electronic records organized in related files is referred to as _____.

17. Information that is stored by individuals on their own disks is called _____.

18. Information that is stored on a network, with files on the network able to be accessed by more than one person at a time is referred to as _____.

19. A roll of film containing a series of frames or images is called _____.

20. A sheet of film containing a series of images arranged in a grid pattern is called _____ _____.

21. The term "COM" is an abbreviation for _____.

22. The term "CAR" is an abbreviation for _____.

23. The term "COLD" is an abbreviation for _____.

24. Software that allows the user to perform a variety of records management functions is referred to as _____.

25. The term "CD-ROM" is an abbreviation for _____.

LANGUAGE SKILLS PRACTICE: PART 4 (CHAPTERS 14–15)

Proofread the following sentences. In the space provided, rewrite the sentences correctly. If you need to review English usage rules, check the Reference Section, pp. 583–599 in your text. Submit your work to your instructor.

DIRECTIONS: The following sentences contain errors in abbreviations; make the necessary corrections.

1. We are reading several books in our English class; ie, Toni Morrison's Beloved, Sandra Cisneros's, The House on Mango Street, and Maya Angelou's Wouldn't Take Nothing for My Journey Now.

   _____

   _____

   _____

2. The C.I.A. performs a vital function for our nation.

   _____

3. Rev. Jones was the minister who presided at the wedding.

   _____

4. The meeting will begin at 10:30 a.m.

   _____

5. Mon. is a holiday.

   _____

DIRECTIONS: The following sentences contain errors in capitalization; correct the sentences.

6. Mary plans to take a course in Management in the fall.

   _____

7. I am reading Tom Clancy's *Debt of Honor*.

   _____

8. We have a cottage on lake Michigan.

   _____

9. The school of medicine at the University of Michigan is considered one of the best in the nation.

   _____

10. The meeting was held at one main place.

   _____

DIRECTIONS: The following sentences contain errors in number usage. Correct the sentences.

11. Almost one hundred people were at the concert, and approximately 50 of those individuals were above 25.

_____

_____

12. The 2000's will bring even greater advances in technology than we have seen in the 1990's.

_____

_____

13. Although she looks much younger, she is almost 80.

_____

14. The 20th century was filled with change.

_____

DIRECTIONS: The following sentences contain errors in plurals and possessives; make the necessary changes.

15. Professors Leiberman's and Kantz's book will be published this spring.

_____

16. The scarf is her's.

_____

DIRECTIONS: Change the following sentences by complying with the proofreaders' marks.

17. The boat was named "the lucky lady."

_____

18. Yes I do plan to attend the graduation ceremony.

_____

19. The individuals will be auditioning for the theatre production that will begin in May.

_____

DIRECTIONS: The following sentences contain misspelled words. Correct the spelling.

20. He is a world traveller.

_____

21. The chair is not useable in my opinion.

_____

22. I am so pleased that you were able to avoid an arguement.

_____

23. He bought potatos, tomatos, and onions at the market.

_____

24. We have been picnicing all day.

_____

25. My day has been unmanagable.

_____

Chapter 16 Supplemental Exercise

DIECTIONS: Your employer, Juan Menendez, leaves you the notes given below. You are to prepare an agenda for the Metropolitan Quality Council meeting. You are to use the agenda form given on the student template disk, file SE16. Submit your completed agenda to your instructor.

From the Desk of . . .
Juan Menendez

The Metropolitan Quality Council meeting is set for Wednesday, April 23, at the Wonderlin Hotel, 919 East Main Street, Detroit. Parking is provided in the Wonderlin Garage. The meeting will be from 11:45 to 1:40. There will also be an Executive Board meeting from 1:50 to 3:00. Lunch will begin at 11:45. Guests will be introduced by Jacqueline Ford at 12:10. Allow five minutes for this activity. The purpose of the meeting is to implement several quality measures, the objectives are: Propose a quality leadership board, outline the elements of an effective Council, present a Latin American Conference, and introduce assessment of the Board.

Mike Clingerfelt will outline how to be an effective council from 12:35-1:00.

Anita Leigh-Purcell will present the Latin-American Conference and suggest a committee organization from 1:00 to 1:20.

Bruce Waldrup will introduce Board assessment from 1:20-1:40 and receive benchmarking ideas.

Jacqueline Ford will adjourn the meeting at 1:40.

The Executive Board meeting will meet from 1:50 to 3:00.

OA17-3 (GOAL 3)

DIRECTIONS: Using the expenses itemized on the following pages, complete the "Individual Trip Expense Report" form given below for Mr. Menendez. Submit the expense

ENTER ONLY ONE AMOUNT PER LINE, PER DAY.

PEOPLE FIRST INTERNATIONAL — INDIVIDUAL TRIP EXPENSE REPORT

NAME ___ SAVE NO. ___ ENDING SPEEDOMETER ___ CHANGED DRIVER'S LICENSE NO. ___ TR. NO. ___

WEEK ENDING ___ SATURDAY ___

	SUNDAY	MONDAY	TUESDAY	WEDNESDAY	THURSDAY	FRIDAY	SATURDAY	TOTALS
PERSONAL								
MOTEL OR HOTEL								
CITY								
STATE								
ROOM CHARGE (ATTACH RECEIPT) 11								
BREAKFAST								
LUNCH								
DINNER								
TOTAL MEALS → 12								
OTHER PERSONAL 13								
TRANSPORTATION AIRFARE, RAIL, OTHER 14								
VEHICLE (*PERSONAL/RENTAL) 15								
OTHER (TAXI, PARKING) 16								
MISCELLANEOUS (EXPLAIN) 17 ENTERTAINMENT								
SUPPLIES/BUSINESS RELATED 18								
MISC. OTHER (EXPLAIN) 19								
TOTAL FOR DAY								EXPENSES
							LESS CASH ADVANCE	21
							ISSUE CHECK	22

EXPLAIN OF ENTERTAINMENT AND MISCELLANEOUS:
*Mileage is calculated at 33.5 cents per mile

TRAVELER'S SIGNATURE ___

```
                 Central Plaza Hotel Receipt

Lodging
1 Single Rm/King; 2 nights @ $83          $166.00
        Tax                                 11.35

Meals
LaCroix Garden Restaurant, 1/21
        Dinner (1)                         $25.75
        Tax/Gratuity                         5.25

Chef Hans Restaurant, 1/22
        Breakfast Buffet (1) @ 12.95       $12.95
        Tax/Gratuity                         2.45

Chef Hans Restaurant, 1/23
        Breakfast (2) Buffet @ 12.95       $25.90
        Tax/Gratuity                         5.10

Parking
Garage Parking; 3 days @ $10               $30.00
```

Tkt #25681

1/21	5.00
1/22	5.00
1/23	5.00
	15.00
Cash	20.00
Change	5.00

Long-Term LotA
Airport Parking

Other expenses

Car rental, Budgett Car Rental
       Daily rate: $46.98 @ 2 days

From the Desk of Juan Menendez

Valet Parking Tips $8.00

Remember to add the airline tkt.

Chapter 17 Supplemental Exercise

DIRECTIONS: Using the Individual Trip Expense Report form given on the following page, create a spreadsheet that can be used to record and calculate monthly travel expenses. Only totals for each category should be recorded on the monthly report. Include the amounts from Mr. Menendez's New York trip. Print a copy of the spreadsheet and submit it to your instructor.

PEOPLE FIRST INTERNATIONAL

INDIVIDUAL TRIP EXPENSE REPORT

ENTER ONLY ONE AMOUNT PER LINE, PER DAY.

NAME

| WEEK ENDING SATURDAY | SAVE NO. | ENDING SPEEDOMETER | | CHANGED DRIVER'S LICENSE NO. | | TR. NO. |

	SUNDAY	MONDAY	TUESDAY	WEDNESDAY	THURSDAY	FRIDAY	SATURDAY	TOTALS
PERSONAL MOTEL OR HOTEL								
CITY								
STATE								
ROOM CHARGE (ATTACH RECEIPT) 11								
BREAKFAST								
LUNCH								
DINNER								
TOTAL MEALS → 12								
OTHER PERSONAL 13								
TRANSPORTATION AIRFARE, RAIL, OTHER 14								
VEHICLE (*PERSONAL/RENTAL) 15								
OTHER (TAXI, PARKING) 16								
MISCELLANEOUS ENTERTAINMENT (EXPLAIN) 17								
SUPPLIES/BUSINESS RELATED 18								
MISC. OTHER (EXPLAIN) 19								
TOTAL FOR DAY								

EXPLAIN OF ENTERTAINMENT AND MISCELLANEOUS:
*Mileage is calculated at 33.5 cents per mile

	EXPENSES
LESS CASH ADVANCE	21
ISSUE CHECK	22

TRAVELER'S SIGNATURE

OA18-2 (GOAL 2)

DIRECTIONS: Your supervisor, Juan Menendez, was recently installed as treasurer of the Atlee Rotary Club. The club's fiscal year is July 1 to June 30.

- Complete a deposit slip on July 7 for the following four membership dues received:

  Currency $100
  #521 $100
  #103 $100
  #466 $100

  A blank deposit slip is on the following page.
- Write checks for the transactions listed on p. 117. Four checks are to be written; the information for writing the checks appears here, with the blank checks following. Date the checks July 10. The carryover balance from last year is $500. In addition, 18 members prepaid their annual dues of $100 in June. Begin the checkbook register with this total.
- On July 31, two members dropped by the office and left checks 301 and 202 for $100 each for their membership dues. Make the necessary deposit; use the deposit slip on p. 116.
- On July 31, Becky Coviello asked for reimbursement for recycling bins and supplies that she purchased for the Environment Committee. Issue Check #1005 to her.

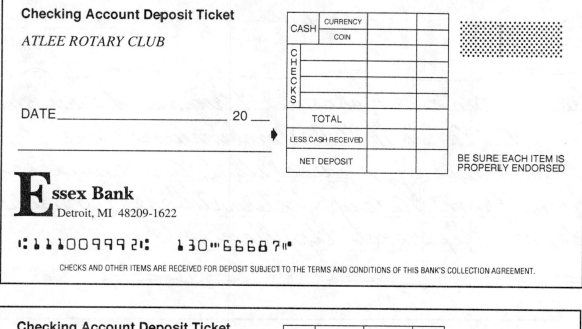

from Cleotha Ketchal, Social Concerns Chairperson
flowers (2 members hospitalized) from Times Square Florist
($45.83) Air Conditioner (for elderly couple) Lipscomb
Appliance ($198.92)

from Kushal Badwar, Business and Professions Chairperson
Printing of speakers Bureau pamphlet by FastPrint ($42.26)

from Duncan English, Citizenship Chairperson
Flag pole (for town entrance) ($112)
U.S. Flag ($55) both purchased from Atlee Hardware

From Blake Kobosius, Programs Chairperson
TV Monitor / VCR Combination Unit
(for viewing videos used by speakers
and from Rotary International) purchased
from Lipscomb Appliance ($176.08)

<table>
<tr><td colspan="2">NO. 1001 $_____</td><td colspan="2">_____ 20__   No. 1001</td></tr>
<tr><td colspan="2">DATE _____ 20 __</td><td colspan="2"></td></tr>
<tr><td colspan="2">TO _____</td><td>PAY TO THE</td><td></td></tr>
<tr><td colspan="2">FOR _____</td><td>ORDER OF_____</td><td>$_____</td></tr>
<tr><td colspan="2">_____</td><td colspan="2">_____ DOLLARS</td></tr>
</table>

	DOLLARS	CENTS
BAL BRG'T FOR'D		
AMT. DEPOSITED		
TOTAL		
AMT. THIS CHECK		
BAL. CAR'D FOR'D		

ATLEE ROTARY CLUB

Essex Bank
Detroit, MI 48209-1622

⑆116009992⑆ 130•66687•

NO. 1002 $ _____

DATE _____ 20 ___

TO _____

FOR _____

_____

	DOLLARS	CENTS
BAL BRG'T FOR'D		
AMT. DEPOSITED		
TOTAL		
AMT. THIS CHECK		
BAL. CAR'D FOR'D		

_____ 20 ___   No. 1002

PAY TO THE
ORDER OF _____ $ _____

_____ DOLLARS

ATLEE ROTARY CLUB

Essex Bank
Detroit, MI 48209-1622

⑆111009992⑆ 130⑈666687⑈

NO. 1003 $ _____

DATE _____ 20 ___

TO _____

FOR _____

_____

	DOLLARS	CENTS
BAL BRG'T FOR'D		
AMT. DEPOSITED		
TOTAL		
AMT. THIS CHECK		
BAL. CAR'D FOR'D		

_____ 20 ___   No. 1003

PAY TO THE
ORDER OF _____ $ _____

_____ DOLLARS

ATLEE ROTARY CLUB

Essex Bank
Detroit, MI 48209-1622

⑆111009992⑆ 130⑈666687⑈

NO. 1004 $ _____

DATE _____ 20 ___

TO _____

FOR _____

_____

	DOLLARS	CENTS
BAL BRG'T FOR'D		
AMT. DEPOSITED		
TOTAL		
AMT. THIS CHECK		
BAL. CAR'D FOR'D		

_____ 20 ___   No. 1004

PAY TO THE
ORDER OF _____ $ _____

_____ DOLLARS

ATLEE ROTARY CLUB

Essex Bank
Detroit, MI 48209-1622

⑆111009992⑆ 130⑈666687⑈

NO. 1005 $ _____

DATE _____ 20 ___

TO _____

FOR _____

_____

	DOLLARS	CENTS
BAL BRG'T FOR'D		
AMT. DEPOSITED		
TOTAL		
AMT. THIS CHECK		
BAL. CAR'D FOR'D		

_____ 20 ___   No. 1005

PAY TO THE
ORDER OF _____ $ _____

_____ DOLLARS

ATLEE ROTARY CLUB

Essex Bank
Detroit, MI 48209-1622

⑆111009992⑆ 130⑈666687⑈

OA18-3 (GOAL 2)

DIRECTIONS: The July statement for the Rotary Club appears below. Using the information given in OA18-3, p. 510 of your text, reconcile the bank statement. Use the form provided on the following page to assist you in the reconciliation.

Complete the instructions given on p. 510 of your text by writing a letter to Essex Bank. Submit your work to your instructor.

Essex Bank
Detroit, MI 48209-1622

ACCT. 130-66687
DATE 8/01/2000
PAGE 1

CHECKING ACCOUNT STATEMENT

ATLEE ROTARY CLUB

BALANCE FORWARD	NO. OF CHECKS	TOTAL CHECKS AND OTHER DEBITS	NO. OF DEP.	TOTAL DEPOSITS AND OTHER CREDITS	BALANCE THIS STATEMENT
2275 00	3	552 26	1	400 00	2122 74

CHECKS AND OTHER DEBITS		DEPOSITS AND OTHER CREDITS	DATE	BALANCE
		400.00	7/7	2,675.00
1001	45.83		7/16	2,629.17
1002	131.43		7/17	2,497.74
1004	375.00		7/22	2,122.74
			7/31	2,122.74

PLEASE EXAMINE AT ONCE
IF NO ERRORS ARE REPORTED
WITHIN 60 DAYS THE ACCOUNT WILL
BE CONSIDERED CORRECT
PLEASE ADVISE US
IN WRITING OF ANY CHANGE
IN YOUR ADDRESS

KEYS TO SYMBOLS

AD	AUTOMATIC DEPOSIT	EC	ERROR CORRECTED
AP	AUTOMATIC PAYMENT	IN	INTEREST
AR	AUTOMATIC REVERSAL	OD	OVERDRAWN
CB	CHARGE BACK	PC	PRINTED CHECKS
CC	CERTIFIED CHECK	RC	RETURN CHECK CHG.
CM	CREDIT MEMO	RT	RETURN ITEM
DM	DEBIT MEMO	SC	SERVICE CHARGE

CHECKING ACCOUNT RECONCILEMENT
Use this form to balance your
checking account.

List checks outstanding (checks written but
not shown on this statement).

CHECK NO.	AMOUNT	
TOTAL OUTSTANDING CHECKS		

IN CASE OF ERRORS OR QUESTIONS ABOUT YOUR STATEMENT

If you think your statement is wrong, or if you need more information about a transaction on your statement, write us as soon as possible on a separate sheet at the address shown on your statement. **We must hear from you no later than 60 days after we sent you the first statement on which the error or problem appeared.** You can telephone us, but doing so will not preserve your rights.

In your letter give us the following information:
1. Your name and account number.
2. The dollar amount of the suspected error.
3. Describe the error and explain, if you can, why you believe there is an error. If you need more information, describe the item you are unsure about.

IN CASE OF ERRORS OR QUESTIONS ABOUT YOUR ELECTRONIC TRANSFERS
TELEPHONE US AT 804-555 -0000/TOLL FREE 1 800 555-0099 OR WRITE US AT P.O. BOX 651, RICHMOND, VA 23225-5223, as soon as you can if you think your statement or receipt is wrong or if you need more information about a transfer listed on the statement or receipt. **We must hear from you no later than 60 days after we sent your FIRST statement on which the problem or error appeared.**

1. Tell us your name and account number.
2. Describe the error or the transfer you are unsure about, and explain as clearly as you can why you believe it is an error or why you need more information.
3. Tell us the dollar amount of the suspected error.

We will investigate your complaint and will correct any error promptly. If we take more than 10 business days to do this, we will recredit your account for the amount you think is in error, so that you will have use of the money during the time it takes to complete our investigation.

IMPORTANT INFORMATION
Information on this statement is being reported to the Internal Revenue Service.

STATEMENT BALANCE	
ADD DEPOSIT MADE BUT NOT SHOWN ON THIS STATEMENT	+
SUBTOTAL	
SUBTRACT TOTAL OUTSTANDING CHECKS	−
TOTAL	

Remember to subtract from your
check register any fees or charges
for printed checks.

This should be the balance in
your check register.

OA18-4 (GOAL 3)

DIRECTIONS: The payroll information on the employees listed below is to be used, along with the information given in your textbook, OA18-4, p. 510, to create a spreadsheet for calculating the weekly payroll. Submit the completed spreadsheet to your instructor.

PAYROLL INFORMATION

Name	Hourly Wage	Withholding	Hospitalization
Robert A. Boone	$ 9.75	9%	$30
Shawn T. Keith	$11.25	10%	$35
Anita S. Kay	$ 8.75	8%	$30
Jose Lane	$ 9.75	9%	$30
Mo Lin	$ 9.25	8%	$30
Isabelle Mark	$ 8.25	8%	$30
Walter A. North	$ 9.75	9%	$35
Quincy E. Park	$ 8.25	8%	$30
Amelia Ramos	$ 9.75	9%	$40
Lisa Stein	$11.25	10%	$35

Chapter 18 Supplemental Exercise

DIRECTIONS: Most daily newspapers in large cities carry financial sections that report stock transactions over-the-counter and on the major stock exchanges, and a variety of Web sites are available on the Internet to provide stock information.

Log into http://www.msn.com. Scroll down the page until you see the stock quotes. Create a table that shows the current stock quotes of the day. Be sure to include columns for the last quote, the change, and the percentage changed. Use another Web site if you prefer, or if you do not have Web access, gather the information from your local newspaper. Print a copy of the table.

VOCABULARY REVIEW: PART 5 (CHAPTERS 16–18)

DIRECTIONS: Complete the sentences below by supplying the correct word(s). Submit a copy to your instructor.

1. A general term applied to a variety of technology-assisted, two-way (interactive) communications via telephone lines, fiber optics, or microwaves is _____.

2. A system of conferencing in which audio and video are transmitted between individuals at distant locations is called _____.

3. When two or more people communicate in real time using only the computer, it is called
    _____.

4. When the ideas and products of a group of people are developed through interaction with each other, it is referred to as _____.

5. An outline of procedures or the order of business to be followed during a meeting is called _____.

6. A physical arrangement of the chairs and tables within a room that allows the leader to have good control of the meeting is _____.

7. A medical condition that results in prolonged periods of fatigue when travelling is referred to as _____.

8. An official government document that certifies the identity and citizenship of an individual and grants the person permission to travel abroad is called _____.

9. A document granted by a government abroad that permits a traveler to enter and travel within a particular country is called _____.

10. A complete travel plan giving the flight numbers or rail numbers (if travelling by train), arrival and departure times, hotel reservations, car rental, and any other pertinent information for a trip is called _____.

11. A multifunction banking machine that allows customers to obtain cash, make deposits, transfer funds, and transact a variety of additional services is called _____.

12. The person or business who orders the bank to pay cash from an account is called _____
    _____.

13. The person or business to whom a check is made payable is called _____.

14. A written signature by the holder of a check for the purpose of transferring ownership is _____.

15. An endorsement that transfers ownership on a check for a specific purpose is _____.

16. A business or personal check that is guaranteed by the bank is _____.

17. A statement showing the financial position of an organization on a certain date is _____ _____.

18. A financial statement that covers the results of the operation of a company for a certain period of time is _____.

19. An instrument that represents shares of ownership in a company is called _____.

20. A financial instrument that promises to pay a definite sum of money at a specified time with interest payable periodically to the holder is called _____.

21. A company that combines the investment funds of many people and in turn invests their funds in a variety of securities is _____.

22. The properties or economic resources owned by an organization are called _____ _____.

23. The debts of an organization are called _____.

24. A check issued by a bank and drawn on the bank's own funds is called _____ _____.

25. When a bank does not return the cancelled checks of an individual or an organization but instead lists the number and amount of the check on the bank statement only, it is called _____.

LANGUAGE SKILLS PRACTICE: PART 5 (CHAPTERS 16–18)

Proofread the following sentences. In the space provided, rewrite the sentences correctly. If you need to review English usage rules, check the Reference Section, pp. 583–599, in your text. Submit your work to your instructor.

DIRECTIONS: The following sentences contain errors in abbreviations; make the necessary corrections.

1. The address of the company is 1125 E. Grand Avenue.

   _____

2. The quarterback has number 18 on his jersey.

   _____

3. He lives on the no. side of Highway 31.

   _____

DIRECTIONS: The following sentences contain errors in capitalization; correct the sentences.

4. Please refer to Page 2 in the book.

   _____

5. Reba Blackshire is the new President-Elect of the organization.

   _____

6. I wrote aunt Patricia and uncle Norris last evening.

   _____

7. We hung new Venetian blinds in our home.

   _____

DIRECTIONS: The following sentences contain errors in number usage. Correct the sentences.

8. The candy bar costs 75.

   _____

9. The train runs this route at 9 p.m. and 12 p.m.

   _____

10. The folder should have 1/2 cut tabs.

   _____

DIRECTIONS: Determine which word or words in parentheses is correct; rewrite the sentence correctly.

11. We will be going to the movie in (a while, awhile).

_____

12. The meeting will be held (at, at about) noon.

_____

13. He graciously (accepted, excepted) the gift.

_____

14. The company is two miles (farther, further).

_____

15. The post is (stationary, stationery)

_____

16. (Who, whom) shall I ask to do the presentation?

_____

DIRECTIONS: The following sentences contain misspelled words. Correct the spelling.

17. My consceince told me that the action was wrong.

_____

18. He droped the ball.

_____

19. The psychologist pointed out that we have difering gifts.

_____

The following words have been divided incorrectly. Correct the word division and provide the rule you followed in dividing the word correctly.

20. ap-ple _____

_____

21. care-lessness _____

_____

22. self-con-trol _____

_____

OA19-1 (GOALS L, 2, AND 3)

DIRECTIONS: Refer to OA19-1 on p. 553 of your text. Then, complete the employment application given below. Submit your work to your instructor.

EMPLOYMENT APPLICATION

People First International

AN EQUAL OPPORTUNITY EMPLOYER

Date of Application _____

PERSONAL INFORMATION

Name of
Applicant _____   Social Security No. _____
             First   Middle   Last

Present Address _____   Phone _____

City _____ State _____ Zip Code _____

Kind of _____   ☐ Full Time   ☐ 1st Shift

Work _____   ☐ Part Time   ☐ 2nd Shift

Desired _____   ☐ Summer   ☐ 3rd Shift

EDUCATIONAL INFORMATION

Type of School	Name and Address	How Many Years Attended	Graduated	Course or Major
Grammar or Grade			☐ Yes ☐ No	
High School			☐ Yes ☐ No	
College			☐ Yes ☐ No	
Postgraduate			☐ Yes ☐ No	
Business or Trade			☐ Yes ☐ No	
Other			☐ Yes ☐ No	

EMPLOYMENT HISTORY

(Please Complete Even if Supplemented by a Resumé)

List Most Recent Position First	MONTHLY SALARY	EMPLOYED FROM	EMPLOYED TO	TOTAL MONTHS

1. Employer _____ $ _____ | | | |

Address _____ REASON FOR LEAVING _____

Name & Title of Supervisor _____ _____

Your Position and Duties _____ _____

_____

2. Employer _____ $ _____ | | | |

Address _____ REASON FOR LEAVING _____

Name & Title of Supervisor _____ _____

Your Position and Duties _____ _____

_____

3. Employer _____ $ _____ | | | |

Address _____ REASON FOR LEAVING _____

Name & Title of Supervisor _____ _____

Your Position and Duties _____ _____

_____

4. Employer _____ $ _____ | | | |

Address _____ REASON FOR LEAVING _____

Name & Title of Supervisor _____ _____

Your Position and Duties _____ _____

_____

5. Employer _____ $ _____ | | | |

Address _____ REASON FOR LEAVING _____

Name & Title of Supervisor _____ _____

Your Position and Duties _____ _____

_____

6. Employer _____ $ _____ | | | |

Address _____ REASON FOR LEAVING _____

Name & Title of Supervisor _____ _____

Your Position and Duties _____ _____

_____

List any other experience that you feel would be significant in our evaluation of your capabilities. Attach an additional sheet if necessary.

_____

_____

_____

_____

In signing this application you hereby authorize the company to conduct investigations including verification of prior employment history and education. Your signature indicates your awareness that false statements or failures to disclose information may be sufficient to disqualify you from employment, or if employed, may result in your dismissal.

_____   _____
Date   Signature of applicant

OA19-2 (GOAL 4)

DIRECTIONS: Refer to OA19-2, p. 553, in your textbook. You, along with three of your classmates, are to conduct a mock interview. The questions for the interview are given in your textbook. Suggestions to help you in answering these questions are given on p. 135. Once you complete the interview, you are to evaluate yourself on the interview. When you complete the evaluation of your classmates, you are to evaluate their interview. Use the form below to evaluate each person who is interviewed.

EVALUATOR FORM

1. What were your general impressions of the interviewee?

2. Did the interviewee have trouble answering any of the questions? If so, what were they?

3. How could the interviewee's answers been better?

4. Did the interviewee appear nervous?

5. Did the interviewee make eye contact with the interviewer?

6. Did the interviewee appear confident?

7. What suggestions would you make to the interviewee to improve his or her performance?

8. What did the interviewee do particularly well?

OA19-2 (GOAL 4)

DIRECTIONS: Use the form below for your self-assessment.

INTERVIEWEE SELF-ASSESSMENT FORM

1. How did I do generally?

2. Were there questions that I had trouble answering? If so, what were they?

3. How could my answers have been better?

4. What mistakes would I correct?

5. What did I do particularly well?

6. Was I nervous?

7. Did I make eye contact with the interviewer?

8. Did I appear confident?

OA19-2 (GOAL 4)

DIRECTIONS: Use this sheet as suggestions for answering the questions you will be asked during the mock interview situation.

SUGGESTIONS FOR ANSWERING INTERVIEW QUESTIONS

- What are your goals?

  Be certain that you know what your goals are. Review your goals before going to the interview. Then, when asked the question, give your goals. Know, however, that if your goals do not match with the position you are seeking, you probably have talked yourself out of a job.

- What are your strengths?

  Choose strengths that will help you get the job. For example, your answer might be technology skills and communications skills for an office professional position in which these skills are stressed. However, do not say that you have these skills unless you do. The point is to pick the strengths that you do have that match the job for which you are applying.

- What are your weaknesses?

  Choose a weakness that is not critical to success on the job or one that relates to content knowledge (something that can be learned) as opposed to a personal quality (which is much more difficult to learn). Make the weaknesses a positive. Talk about what you are doing to correct your weaknesses. Give specific examples of what you are doing.

- What do you know about the company?

  Find out as much information as you can before going on the interview. Relay the information in a concise manner. For example, you might say something such as, "I have learned that one of the company directions in the next five years is to become a leader in the software field."

- Why do you think you are qualified for this position?

  Identify the job requirements that were advertised for the position; talk about the skills you have that meet these job requirements. Give specific examples of your work experience or your educational experience that demonstrate that you have the skills.

- Why did you leave your previous job?

  Be truthful; put your answers in a positive light. For example, if there was a downsizing, you might say that the department was phased out due to company downsizing. If you left because you are interested in a more challenging position, say that you are interested in a company where there are greater growth opportunities than you had with your previous company. Show that you attempted to make it better. For example, you might say that you had several conversations with your supervisor about the department's directions and the possibility for growth. You might also say that you suggested ways in which your job might be altered to provide for growth.

- Do you have any questions?

Before you go on the interview, think through questions that you might ask. Do not ask anything that you should already know. Ask questions pertaining to the position, the organization, and/or the next steps in the hiring process. Do not ask questions about salary and benefits at this point. Here are some possible questions:

To whom would I report?
What is a typical career path for this position?
What qualities are needed for success in this position?
What are the biggest challenges facing the organization/department for the next two years?
How would you describe the working environment in the organization/department?

Chapter 19 Supplemental Exercise

DIRECTIONS: Conduct the following interviews. Prepare a short report on the answers given by the people being interviewed. Identify the individuals you interviewed and give their company affiliation. Submit your report to your instructor.

- Interview an individual who has recently changed jobs. Learn why the change was made and what steps were taken regarding the change in employment. Ask the interviewee what he or she learned from the experience.

- Interview a supervisor; ask the person the following:
  – In your experience, what contributes to employees losing their jobs?
  – What can employees do to enhance their growth potential?

OA20-2 (GOALS 1 AND 3)

DIRECTIONS: Rate yourself on your leadership potential. Also ask one of your class-mates to rate you. Two copies of the "Leadership Rating Scale" are provided—one for your self-evaluation and one for your classmate's rating of you. Talk with the classmate about how he or she feels you might improve. Write a short report on ways that you think you can improve your leadership skills. Submit your work to your instructor.

LEADERSHIP RATING SCALE

The statements below are intended to make you aware of your leadership potential. If you are working, answer them based on your work experience. If you are not working, answer them based on your experiences in school or in organizations to which you belong. Respond to the statement by placing a check mark in the proper column. Be as honest as you possibly can when rating yourself. To be an effective leader, most of your answers should be in the "Always" column

		Always	*Sometimes*	*Never*
1.	I listen to others and encourage them to express their views.			
2.	I provide others with complete and accurate information.			
3.	I encourage teamwork.			
4.	I establish measurable objectives and goals.			
5.	I handle mistakes in a way that allows others to learn and grow.			
6.	I expect others to perform well without close supervision.			
7.	I am sensitive to the accomplishments of others and give recognition for good performance.			
8.	I delegate work.			
9.	I am aware of my wants, needs, and values.			
10.	I look for creative solutions to problems.			
11.	I make an effort to keep up-to-date on developments in my area of responsibility.			
12.	I evaluate others on their job performance.			
13.	I find it easy to communicate with people.			
14.	I set work standards after seeking input from others.			
15.	I believe it is necessary to set priorities.			
16.	I am consistent.			
17.	I evaluate others based on my experiences with them.			
18.	I am usually flexible.			
19.	I like to learn new skills.			
20.	I articulate the objectives that I expect of others.			

DIRECTIONS: Rate your classmate on his or her leadership skills using the form below. Respond to the statement by placing a check mark in the proper column. Be as honest and objective as you possibly can when rating your classmate.

LEADERSHIP RATING SCALE

	Always	*Sometimes*	*Never*
1. Listens to others and encourages them to express their views.	_____	_____	_____
2. Provides others with complete and accurate information.	_____	_____	_____
3. Encourages teamwork.	_____	_____	_____
4. Establishes measurable objectives and goals.	_____	_____	_____
5. Handles mistakes in a way that allows others to learn and grow.	_____	_____	_____
6. Expects others to perform well without close supervision.	_____	_____	_____
7. Is sensitive to the accomplishments of others and gives recognition for good performance.	_____	_____	_____
8. Delegates work.	_____	_____	_____
9. Is aware of own wants, needs, and values.	_____	_____	_____
10. Looks for creative solutions to problems.	_____	_____	_____
11. Makes an effort to keep up-to-date on developments in own area of responsibility.	_____	_____	_____
12. Evaluates others on their job performance.	_____	_____	_____
13. Finds it easy to communicate with people.	_____	_____	_____
14. Sets work standards after seeking input from others.	_____	_____	_____
15. Believes it is necessary to set priorities.	_____	_____	_____
16. Is consistent.	_____	_____	_____
17. Evaluates others based on own experiences with them.	_____	_____	_____
18. Is usually flexible.	_____	_____	_____
19. Likes to learn new skills.	_____	_____	_____
20. Articulates the objectives expected of others.	_____	_____	_____

CHAPTER 20 SUPPLEMENTAL EXERCISE

DIRECTIONS: Select four to six of your classmates to work with on this case. Respond to the questions below the case. Be prepared to discuss the case with the entire class.

The workgroup team consists of five employees, with one supervisor (a male). The male was promoted to the supervisory position (after being part of the workgroup) eight months ago. Before his promotion, the group worked extremely well together. The previous supervisor was very supportive. The morale in the group was high and productivity was excellent. In the last six months, the group has had major problems. One employee has had a series of personal problems that have affected her work. She has been absent frequently due to the problems. Two employees have been quarreling over work assignments, and the production of both employees has decreased drastically. One employee is habitually late and extends his lunch hour by 10 to 15 minutes every day. The division manager has complained to the supervisor that productivity is down and that other employees are complaining that the department is late in meeting its deadlines.

The new supervisor has this philosophy about people.

• People are lazy and dislike working.

• People must be controlled and disciplined to get them to perform their jobs.

• The average person has little ambition.

1. Is there a problem with the supervisor? If so, what is it and how should it be handled?

2. What are the problems in the workgroup? How should they be handled?

VOCABULARY REVIEW: PART 6 (CHAPTERS 19–20)

DIRECTIONS: Complete the sentences below by supplying the correct word(s). Submit a copy to your instructor.

1. The process of identifying and establishing a group of acquaintances, friends, and even relatives who can assist you in the job search process is called _____.

2. A concise statement of your background, education, skills, and experience used in the job search process is called _____.

3. A compilation of samples of your work is called _____.

4. Interviewing an employee any place and at any time using technology is called _____ _____.

5. A letter written after an interview to thank the person for the interview is referred to as _____.

6. Formal evaluations of individuals on a job are called _____.

7. The state of being bound emotionally or intellectually to some course of action is referred to as _____.

8. When leaving a job, many companies ask that employees complete _____.

9. The process of persuading others to take action that is consistent with the purpose of the leader or the group's shared purposed is referred to as _____.

10. The ability to act is called _____.

11. Allowing employees to take on more responsibility is called _____.

12. In planning, the process of taking ideas from strategic thinking and translating them into an action format is called _____.

13. The process of making detailed decisions about who will accomplish the objectives, how and when they will be accomplished, who will be accountable, what resources are needed, and how they will be evaluated is called _____.

14. Preparing a list of the tasks for a specific job and the personal characteristics necessary to perform the task successfully are referred to as _____.

15. The process of entrusting the performance of some specific work to another person is called _____.

LANGUAGE SKILLS PRACTICE: PART 6 (CHAPTERS 19–20)

Proofread the following sentences. In the space provided, rewrite the sentences correctly. If you need to review English usage rules, check the Reference Section, pp. 583–599, in your text. Submit your work to your instructor.

DIRECTIONS: The following sentences contain errors in abbreviations; make the necessary corrections.

1. Our office hours are from 8:30 am to 5 pm.

   _____

2. Doctor J. T. Adams will deliver the commencement address.

   _____

3. Rev. Frakes will provide the invocation for the dinner on Tues.

   _____

DIRECTIONS: The following sentences contain errors in capitalization; correct the sentences.

4. He observes yom kippur, a jewish holiday.

   _____

5. St. louis and Kansas city are being considered as possible sites for the next convention.

   _____

6. Hugh Baker was recently promoted to Vice President of Minor Pharmaceuticals.

   _____

7. The title of the book is *Procedures for The Office Professional*.

   _____

DIRECTIONS: The following sentences contain errors in number usage. Correct the sentences.

8. The laser printer will cost $500.00, but the cabinet will be several hundred dollars less.

   _____

9. I will see you at eight a.m. tomorrow.

   _____

10. The ratio of lecture hours to laboratory hours for most science courses is one to three.

    _____

DIRECTIONS: Select the correct word from those shown in parentheses.

11. (Accept, Except) my (compliments, compliments) for a job well done.

_____

12. The temperature was cold much (farther, further) south than we expected.

_____

13. Since (its, it's) record is good, I bought the stock.

_____

14. Only 50 (percent, per cent) of the amount has been paid.

_____

15. The stock list did not include diskettes or (stationary, stationery).

_____

DIRECTIONS: The following sentences contain errors in plurals and possessives; make the necessary corrections.

16. A number of CPA attended the conference.

_____

17. Her brother's-in-law property joins mine.

_____

18. The people's hopes are optimistic.

_____

DIRECTIONS: The following sentences are punctuated incorrectly. Make the necessary changes.

19. The speaker said "The power that moves individuals is enthusiasm".

_____

20. Have you read the article Ten Tips for the Effective Manager?

_____

21. What a scene.

_____

22. Did the employment counselor say "Learn all you can about the company before your interview."

_____

23. Jill Baugham the sales associate in your region will be calling you next week.

_____

24. Louisville Kentucky and Knoxville Tennessee are all on our itinerary.

_____

DIRECTIONS: The following sentences contain misspelled words. Correct the spelling.

25. The last seen of the play depicted an accident in which the main character was lieing unconscience in the street.

_____

26. My conscious was clear; though I still felt embarrased to be part of the group.

_____

27. It was as tho they had been repremanded in front of the hole world!

_____

DIRECTIONS: The following words have been divided incorrectly. In the space provided, show the correct word division and provide the rule you followed in dividing the word correctly.

28. radi-ation _____

    Rule _____

29. re-ctify _____

    Rule _____

30. mon-itor _____

    Rule _____

31. forestal-ling _____

    Rule _____

SIMULATED OFFICE APPLICATION

Day 1—Tuesday, April 11

DIRECTIONS: When you arrive at work, you discover that Mr. Menendez worked late last evening and left several items for you on your email; check your email on the student template disk in the file SOA1a. After reviewing all the tasks, prioritize them and use the form SOA2 below to list the order in which you will complete the tasks. Delegate the filing, setting up of appointments, and keying the report to your assistant. Determine the order in which these tasks should be accomplished and when. Discuss this order with your assistant. Use the Internet in determining flight times; company policy dictates that you fly coach class.

The fax number for the Paris office is 30 (0) 1 43 56 55 77. A fax cover sheet is on the student template disk in file OA13-2. A memorandum form is on the student template disk in file OA02-1b. In addition to the tasks given here, you need to compose three letters that Mr. Menendez asked you to write last Friday; he needs them by noon today. (You will not write the letters for this simulation; your task is to determine what priority they are to take.) Also, you need to begin planning a two-day conference for the IAAP on Effective Communication. The conference will be held in October. You want to have a first draft of your proposal to the president of IAAP for review in May. Information about the conference will need to be sent out to all members by the last of June. Determine if there are some tasks that you can delegate to Roger for IAAP.

SOA2

TO BE DONE	TO BE DELEGATED
1. _____	1. _____
2. _____	2. _____
3. _____	3 _____.
4. _____	4. _____
5. _____	5. _____
6. _____	6. _____

Day 2—Wednesday, April 12

DIRECTIONS: This morning Mr. Menendez asked you for a copy of a letter that was written to the Frankfurt office two weeks ago. When you check the file, it is not there. You then asked Roger if he has it. He says he doesn't know. When you gave him the filing yesterday, you asked that it be completed before he left work yesterday. You were upset with his answer, but you didn't have time to talk then. You merely asked him for the materials to be filed and looked through them. You found the letter and took it to Mr. Menendez.

Problems have been building with Roger, and you know that you need to sit down and talk with him. However, you have not taken the time to do so. Here are some of the problems that have occurred.

- Roger is at least 15 minutes late for work once a week; several times he has been 30 minutes late. He has given you no explanation for his lateness.
- Roger can never seem to find anything in the file.
- Roger spends about 30 minutes each day in chitchat with Paul, one of the office professionals.
- Roger's attitude is not always good; several times he has seemed upset when you have given him a large amount of work. He doesn't say anything, but he walks away in a huff and barely speaks to you for the remainder of the day.

During the six months of Roger's employment, you have not sat down with him to review his job performance. In fact, you have never told him how he will be evaluated. You know that you are not handling the situation correctly, but you have never supervised an employee before and you feel inadequate in the role. You decide to talk with one of your coworkers who supervises three people and is highly respected for her leadership skills. She advises you that you must talk with Roger immediately. She also tells you that you must give him a detailed explanation of how he will be evaluated. You decide that you will design an evaluation form before you talk with him. You also decide that you will make a detailed outline of what you will talk with him about and how you should handle each situation. Prepare the evaluation form and the outline.

Day 3—Thursday, April 13

- Mr. Menendez asks that you compose two letters for his signature. One letter is to be written to Dr. Edwina Bos, Lamboa Corporation, 713 Tulip Lane, Farminton Hills, MI 48331, asking her to speak at the Detroit Economic Conference to be held on December 10 of this year on directions for the Detroit Public Schools. The presentation should be no more than one hour in length, with the time frame being from 10 a.m. to 11 a.m. The second letter is to be written to a new client, Mr. Wayne Grant, Remien, Inc., 7501 Eagle Drive, Detroit, MI 48234, thanking him for his business and suggesting a luncheon meeting on Tuesday, May 2, at Brookhaven Country Club to discuss any training needs that he might have. Prepare the letters using the letterhead on the student template disk in file OA10-3.
- You have your talk with Roger, going over his performance and giving him a copy of the evaluation form that you developed. He listens to your comments and responds. He assures you that he appreciates your talking with him and that he will do a better job in the future. After the meeting, you notice that he has a long conversation with his friend Paul. You wonder if he is discussing his evaluation. Should you talk with Roger? Note how you should handle the situation.

Day 4—Friday, April 14

- Your morning begins with a call at 9:05 a.m. from a client. He is upset and complains loudly about the lack of service he is getting from People First. You listen to what he has to say and then suggest that you will have Mr. Menendez get back with him. You explain that Mr. Menendez is not expected in until approximately 11:00 a.m. He informs you that he wants to talk with "someone in charge" immediately. You refer his call to Ms. Bauer, Director of Human Resources. After Ms. Bauer talks with him, she gives you a call telling you that she needs to see Mr. Menendez as soon as he comes in. You send an email to Mr. Menendez about the situation. Write the email; prepare your own email form. Mr. Menendez comes in at 11:05 a.m. and goes to his office, shutting the door behind him. You decide that he doesn't want to be disturbed so you do not bother him with any messages. At 11:30 a.m., Ms. Bauer comes in (quite upset) and asks if you have told Mr. Menendez that she must see him. You respond that you sent him an email; she tells you she must talk with him immediately and knocks on his door. After she leaves, Mr. Menendez tells you that you should have told him about the need to talk with Ms. Bauer. How should you respond to Mr. Menendez?
- At 1 p.m., Ms. Engleton (a supervisor with People First) calls for some information that you have in your files. You ask her to hold while you pull the information. As you start toward the files, you are interrupted by Mr. Menendez with an urgent matter. When you get back to the phone (approximately two minutes later) Ms. Engleton has hung up. She calls back in five minutes and angrily tells you that she needs the information. How should you have handled the situation?
- At 2 p.m. you pass the copier and notice that Roger is making copies of articles from periodicals. You ask him why he is copying the articles and he responds, "I need them for my class tonight." You have had a bad day, so you decide you will think about how to handle the situation and talk with him tomorrow. Make a note of what you should say to Roger.
- You need to research effective communication techniques—both verbal and written—to get some ideas about what you want to recommend for the IAAP Effective Communications Conference. You decide to look for sources on the Internet. Select two or three Internet sources and prepare a tentative program for the IAAP Conference. You do not have the time to do this during working hours so you decide to stay late to work on it. Who should you inform that you are working late and what precautions should you take?

Day 5—Monday, April 17

- At 9:30 a.m., one of the office professionals from another department calls with an urgent matter that she needs to discuss with you. She tells you that she cannot discuss it over the phone and must see you. You know that she is a conscientious employee and is not easily upset. You tell her to come over. She asks that you meet her in Conference Room A; she does not want anyone in the office to see her enter your office. You agree to meet her and ask that Roger cover the phones while you are away. The employee, Debra, tells you that one of the men in her office has been making suggestive remarks to her for weeks. She has just laughed at him and continued on with her work. Today, he encountered her in the hall and told her that he is not "kidding." He said that he finds her very attractive and suggested that he knows she finds him attractive also. He suggested that they meet at a hotel this evening. He also tells her that he can make it difficult for her at People First if she refuses him. She is so upset that she says nothing; she just turns and walks away. As she does, he calls out with a laugh, "I'll be waiting for your answer." She doesn't know how to handle the situation and asks for your advice. What should she do? Explain what advice you give her.

When you get back in the office (after about an hour), Mr. Menendez tells you that he has been looking for you, and Roger has no idea where you are. What should you tell Mr. Menendez? How should you have handled the situation with Roger? Should you have told Roger where you were going?

- At 2 p.m. you have a talk with Roger about the "copying incident" from yesterday. When you tell him that it is not appropriate to make copies for his class on the People First copier, he says he does not understand why. He tells you that he knows that you make copies of material for IAAP on the copier. He doesn't see the difference. His continued education is professional growth for him; he plans to get a bachelor's degree in engineering. What is your response to Roger?

Submit all written materials to your instructor; these materials are:

Day 1—Tuesday, April 11

- To-do list
- Itinerary for Paris
- Memorandum to Jean in the Paris office, along with the fax cover sheet
- Determination of whether or not you can delegate tasks to Roger for IAAP

Day 2—Wednesday, April 12

- Evaluation form for Roger
- Outline of discussion with Roger about job performance

Day 3—Thursday, April 13

- Two letters—one to Dr. Bos and one to Mr. Grant
- How you should handle the situation on Thursday, April 13, when Roger talks with his friend

Day 4—Friday, April 14

- Email to Mr. Menendez
- Response to Mr. Menendez about the handling of the situation with the difficult caller
- How the telephone call at 1 p.m. with Ms. Engleton should have been handled
- How you should respond to Roger about copying materials for his class
- Tentative program for the IAAP Seminar
- Precautions you should take when working late; who should be notified about working late

Day 5—Monday, April 17

- Advice you gave to Debra
- Response to Mr. Menendez on the situation; what Roger should have been told about the situation
- Response to Roger on his question about your making copies for IAAP and his not being allowed to make copies for his class